ISBN: 979-8-9874811-4-1

How to Use A New Path

We're glad you've picked up *A New Path: A Guide to the Challenges and Opportunities After Deportation.* Deportation can be scary. You might be sad about leaving friends and family in the US. It's normal to be worried about the future. Perhaps you are a family member or friend of someone who is facing deportation. Maybe you plan to move to your home country to be with a loved one who is being deported. Maybe you want to move to your home country so you won't have to worry about deportation.

No matter what group you fall into, this guide can help you. It can help you by giving you information about what to expect while you're being deported. It also can help you build a new life in your country of origin by giving you advice about employment, government programs, meeting your basic needs, and more.

Know your rights! Deportation is not a given. You have the right to fight your deportation. This guide also includes legal resources and organizations that can help you with that process.

We use the term "home country" to mean the country you might be deported to. We understand that country may not feel like home. You may have no memories of it. You may not even speak the language. We do not mean that it is your rightful home or that you feel connected to it. We are only using that term to distinguish it from the U.S. You may also see the term "country of origin" which means the same thing.

There Are Five Main Sections in *A New Path*:

- **Preparing for Possible Deportation**
  Information that will help you fight and/or get ready for deportation or return.
- **After Your Return**
  Information about how to set up your life in your home country. It has information on meeting basic needs, finding a job, school, and more.
- **Healing and Moving Forward**
  Advice on healing, mindfulness and having healthy relationships.
- **Deportation to Central America**
  Resources for return to Guatemala, Honduras and El Salvador, including a directory of resources in each country.
- **Directory and Additional Resources**
  Contact information for useful resources in the US and other countries. It also has helpful forms you can tear out and use.

Let's be honest: deportation is difficult. You may feel angry if you are being deported against your will. If you are leaving behind family and friends, you may also be sad about separating from people you love. It may not feel fair that you or your loved one is forced to leave the country.

All of these feelings are appropriate.

At the same time, we encourage you to make plans so that you are prepared. Some recently deported people only want to return to the US. They don't think about building a new life in their new country. This will make things even harder for you.

Some advantages you might have returning to your home country after living in the US:

- You likely have some knowledge of English. Even if you are not a strong speaker, speaking some English is very good. Employers are looking for English-speaking people and may even pay for you to attend classes.
- If you have a criminal record in the US it's unlikely to follow you to Mexico.
- Your knowledge of US culture may also help you to get some jobs in Mexico.

A New Path will help you meet challenges and use your skills. We wouldn't have written it if we didn't believe in you. Don't stop believing in yourself. In this book you'll find supportive words from people who have been deported. Some of them are alumni of the Education Justice Project, a college-in-prison program at Danville Correctional Center in Illinois. We're thankful for their help with the guide and hope you find their words helpful.

Remember, others have successfully handled deportation, and you can, too. Take the time to read this guide, make plans, and seek help from others. This guide contains information about many organizations that can help you. Don't be afraid to reach out to them for help. You might even be able to join these organizations to advocate for others who also face deportation. And don't give up!

Please keep in touch. We want to know about your experience, and hear your ideas about how we can improve the guide. We may also be able to connect you with resources in your home country. Please write to us at unnuevocamino@educationjustice.net.

We wish you the best on this new journey in your life.

In solidarity,
The Education Justice Project

About *A New Path*

A New Path was written and produced by the Education Justice Project (EJP). EJP is part of the College of Education at the University of Illinois. Since 2008, EJP has taught college courses to people at Danville Correctional Center in Central Illinois.

A New Path started because we care about people like you who live with the threat of deportation. The guide is made by a group of committed EJP members called the Reentry Guide Initiative.

We don't believe that people should be detained and deported. The publication of this book should not be seen as an endorsement of deportation. The fact is that every year thousands of people are deported. We created this resource so that those individuals who face deportation can have the information and resources they need for a successful transition.

☆ DISCLAIMER

We have listed a lot of programs, services, and businesses throughout this guide as resources for people returning to their home country. We don't endorse any of these organizations. We also don't guarantee that these resources will be helpful (although we certainly hope they are). The world is changing all the time. That means we can't be sure that information in the guide is current. We've tried to use the best, most up-to-date information from trusted sources.

Request Our Guides!

Returning to live in the United States after release from prison or jail? Please request a copy of *Mapping Your Future: A Guide to Successful Reentry,* also produced by the Education Justice Project. Both *Mapping Your Future* and *A New Path* are available in English and Spanish and can be ordered the following ways:

- reentryillinois.net
- (217) 300-5150
- reentry@educationjustice.net
- Education Justice Project
  1001 S Wright St
  Champaign, IL 61820

Cost

Each copy of *A New Path* costs around $9 to print and send. We provide free copies of *A New Path* to those who need it. If you or your organization are able to pay for copies of this guide, this will allow us to provide more guides for those who are unable to purchase them. To purchase guides, please send a check for the amount of the guides you would like to purchase to the address above.

Acknowledgments

The 2023-2024 edition of *A New Path* was revised and authored by the following individuals:

- Lee Ragsdale, Director, Reentry Guide Initiative
- Linda Larsen, Research and Writing Coordinator, Reentry Guide Initiative
- Manpreet Gurtatta, Distribution & Outreach Coordinator, Reentry Guide Initiative

Advisory Committee: Michael Cannon, Ricky Hamilton, Martice Hanible, Josephine Horace, Roberto Lazcano, Pablo Mendoza, Fatima Monteiro, Douglas Taylor, David Todd, and Kilroy Watkins.

***A New Path* Research Team:** Daniela Barbosa, Lili Burciaga, Natalia Fic, Xochitl Guerrero, Linda Larsen, Mariama Mwilambwe, Lee Ragsdale, and Amber Scarborough.

RGI Members: Daniela Barbosa, Kathy Bauer, Tyeese Braslavsky, Lili Burciaga, Sarah Dodoo, Xochitl Guerrero, Leanne Knobloch, Negar Mehr, Kendra Mills, Mariama Mwilambwe, Andi Quasebarth Lee, Sydney Sakharia, Amber Scarborough, Ira Shinn, MoDena Stinnette, Jazmine Thompson, Katia Rodriguez, Andrea DaViera, Elise Duwe, Leanne Knolboch, Lis Pollock, Gill Snyder and Anya de la Vega.

RGI Interns: Tyla Allen, Christy Cannon, Catherine Cabrera, Sarah Coffman, Xosa Cox, Kelsie Haseltine, Kaylee Janakos, Maya Korol, and Alina Loewenstein.

Designers: Ashley Jung, Jack Johnson, Jamarri Nix, Surface 51.

Special thanks to:
Beth Pearl, Editor
Rebecca Ginsburg, EJP Director
Jamie Hines, EJP Operations Director
The Mexican Consulate of Chicago, Office of Protection
Immigration Unit Pilot at the Law Office of the Cook County Public Defender
Freedom for Immigrants

We would also like to thank EJP alumni and other deported/returned people and systems-impacted individuals who have contributed to the guide: Alex A., Alex V., Austin C., Brian N., Chris H., Darrell W., Dennis M., Earl W., Edmund B., Erick N., Flori L., Greg A., Heather B., Israel G., Jennifer V., Jobie T., Johnny P., Joseph B., Julia B., Katerina B., Keke, Marlon C., Mike T., Missy L., Orlando M., Oscar S., Ramon C., Roberto B., Roberto L., Shaun W., Tony C., Tyrone M.

Thanks as well to those who contributed images: Garifus Garcia, EJP alumni, Alex Vergara, and members of the Facebook Deportee Wives Club.

Common Myths About Deportation

What kind of information will you find in this guide? For one thing, it will show you that some common myths you might have heard aren't true. Here are a few of those myths.

If ICE comes to our door, we have to let them in.

False. Ask to see a warrant signed by a judge, not an immigration official. If they do not have that, you don't have to let them enter your home. See the Know Your Rights chapter.

There is no way to plan for a possible deportation.

False. There are things you can do to have more control over your situation. See the Make a Plan chapter.

You will have fewer opportunities in Mexico than you did in the US.

False. It is true that many Mexicans move to the US for opportunities. But there are a lot of good things about living in Mexico. Opening a small business is much easier and cheaper. If you speak English you will be able to get a lot of jobs. See the Employment chapter to find out more.

Mexico is a dangerous country and my life will be at risk living there.

False. It's true that some parts of Mexico have very high crime rates. The border in particular can be dangerous. Other areas are safer. People who live there learn to live in a safe way. The US State Department issues travel warnings to Americans traveling to Mexico. This may be worth looking at. Many Mexican states have a Level 2 travel warning, meaning "Exercise Increased Caution." These states include Mexico City, Aguascalientes, Baja California Sur, Chiapas, Hidalgo, Oaxaca, San Luis Potosí, Puebla, Querétaro, Tabasco, Tlaxcala, Quintana Roo, Veracruz and Nuevo León. Other Mexican states are labeled as "Reconsider Travel" (Level 3). Others are labeled "Do Not Travel" (Level 4), including Tamaulipas, Sinaloa, Michoacán, Guerrero and Colima. Mexico is unfortunately more dangerous for LGBTQ people than the US.

If I haven't lived in Mexico since I was a child, I won't fit in and will have a very hard time.

False. It is true that it may be easy to tell that you've lived in the US. But you can learn about the culture and ways of your community. Knowing these things can help you fit in. For more information about culture see the Cultural Encounters chapter.

If you have a criminal record in the US it will make it hard for you to get a job in Mexico.

It depends on the employer and where you are. A Mexican company in the south of the country, for example, will probably not do a background check. But a US factory near the border probably will. For more information about looking for jobs and what to do when you have a criminal record, turn to the Employment section. The Directory also has employment resources, with lists of places you can go for help.

Table of Contents

3. Healing and moving forward

4. Deportation to Central America

5. Directory

5. Additional resources

Part 1: Preparing for Possible Deportation

- Living with the Threat of Deportation
- Know Your Rights
- Plan for Possible Deportation
- Getting Help to Fight Your Case
- Preparing for Life in Your Home Country
- At the Border

Living with the Threat of Deportation

Living in the US with the threat of deportation comes with a great deal of anxiety and fear. Part of that anxiety comes from uncertainty: You don't know when or if you will encounter ICE or police. You don't know what might happen to your children if you are arrested. You don't know what life will be like if you are forced to return to your home country.

Knowing what to expect can take away some of the anxiety and stress. This guide gives you an idea of what to expect in an ICE raid, during your time in ICE custody, at the border, and immediately after deportation. See the chapter, Know Your Rights: ICE Encounters and the Removal Process, to learn more about the removal process, from arrest to possible deportation.

Making a plan can also help reduce anxiety and stress. A plan can guide you through the crisis and help you remain calm. It can be hard to think and make decisions under stress but if you've laid out a plan, this will help. The Make a Plan chapter addresses how you can prepare.

This chapter covers ways you can cope mentally with the uncertainty, anxiety and stress. It also addresses some things you may worry about if you are undocumented, like whether you can get a driver's license or medical care.

It covers the following topics:

- Practice patience and mindfulness
- Prepare mentally for challenges
- Getting medical care
- Getting help if you are a victim of a crime
- Driving while undocumented
- Housing protections

> *"Best thing that can reduce anxiety is to have a plan. You don't have to be rigid with that plan, because you're going to ... get out and realize that the world isn't what you expected it to be."*
> **—Joe Joe M.**

Practice Patience and Mindfulness

You are under a lot of stress. Give yourself permission to accept that things may not be ideal or easy. It will be useful to practice patience. Go slow. Breathe. It is natural to feel stressed sometimes, but there are ways of managing your stress and preventing it from getting out of hand.

Think about what you can do to set your mind at ease. What are the hobbies you enjoy? You might play soccer, take long walks, or garden, for example. How can you build such activities into your life to relieve some of the stress?

If you have a daily meditation, mindfulness or exercise routine, maintain it. If not, think about starting one. This will help calm you and allow you to reduce your stress and maintain focus. The chapter on Mindfulness provides detailed guidance on getting started and even has a few guided meditations

Prepare for Mentally for Challenges

As you consider your potential deportation, work on practicing patience, both with others and with yourself.

What skills do you use to manage stress?

When things go wrong, or when you're disappointed, what can you do to keep yourself on track and focused?

What have you done in the past to successfully adjust to major life changes?

What skills, habits, or traits helped you to stay motivated, build positive relationships, and maintain self-respect?

Who can you turn to when you are stressed or anxious? Who is in your support network?

What organizations can be part of your support network? Do you have a church community? Is there an organization that supports people like you?

> *Take a breath. You're going to be in for a ride, and you better pack your patience.*
>
> **—Pablo M.**

Getting Medical Care

If you or a family member are undocumented, you may be afraid to get medical care. Maybe you are afraid they will ask about your immigration status. You may worry about paying for medical bills, especially if you don't have insurance. You have the right to get medical care without worrying about being deported. Health care workers should not ask you questions about your immigration status, nor should they report you to ICE.

You will likely be asked to pay for services out of pocket. Always ask about the expected costs before receiving a service. Look for community health centers that provide low-cost health care and services on a sliding scale.

You can safely get medical care at these places:

- Community health centers that provide low-cost health care: https://www.healthcare.gov/community-health-centers/
- Federally-qualified health centers: https://findahealthcenter.hrsa.gov/
- Urgent care clinics
- Public hospitals
- Emergency rooms
- Safety-net hospitals

If you are undocumented, you cannot enroll in Medicaid, Medicare, or the Children's Health Insurance Program (CHIP) and you also can't get insurance through the Affordable Care Act (ACA) marketplace.

There are some insurance options, though.

- **Insurance through your employer.** You may be eligible to receive insurance through an employer.
- **State programs.** Some states have insurance options for people who are undocumented. Illinois' All Kids program provides affordable healthcare for children of low-income families, regardless of immigration status.
- **Emergency Medicaid.** If you are experiencing a life-threatening emergency, you can apply for Emergency Medicaid to cover the costs. Different states have different ways to apply. Ask a healthcare professional to help you.

If mental health challenges or substance abuse are preventing you from functioning well or feeling good, get help from a mental health professional. If you are feeling especially bad or feel like you might be a danger to yourself or someone else, get help right away. Call the suicide and crisis lifeline at 988 or anonymously contact the Crisis Text Line. The Crisis Text Line provides free, 24/7, confidential support (in English and Spanish) via text message to people in crisis when they text the word HOME to 741741.

You can also call 911 or visit an emergency room if you are in crisis.

Even if you are not in crisis, don't delay getting help if you are feeling depressed, anxious, or angry. If you aren't feeling well mentally and emotionally, it makes it so much harder to move forward in positive and productive ways. When you are feeling mentally healthy, you will find that things will seem more manageable and you'll feel more hopeful.

It may help to find a therapist who works with the undocumented community. See https://www.informedimmigrant.com/resource-type/therapist-directories/ for a directory. There are many low-cost community health clinics where you can get help.

A mental health professional can help you:

- Work through changing harmful behaviors.
- Avoid alcohol or drugs to ease depression and anxiety.
- Feel stronger as you face challenges.
- Come up with goals and plans to solve your problems.
- Identify how your ways of thinking are influencing how you feel.

Mental health professionals can help you decide if it would be a good idea to take medicine to treat your mental disorder, and they can offer treatment for drug and alcohol addictions.

Getting Help if You Are a Victim of a Crime

Many immigrants worry that if they report a crime, they may be deported. But there are laws that can protect you depending on what type of crime you've been a victim of.

- **The Violence Against Women Act** protects victims of domestic violence who are the child, parent or current/former spouse of a US citizen or permanent resident (green card holder) and are abused by the US citizen or permanent resident. If this applies to you, you may be eligible to apply for a green card yourself, without needing help from the person who has abused you.
- **U Nonimmigrant Visa Status** is a protection for people who have been victims of serious crimes and have information about the crime that they want to share with police. This applies only to certain criminal activity and you must be willing to participate in the investigation. Check with your local legal services clinic if you think this may apply to you.
- **T Nonimmigrant Visa Status** is for victims of human trafficking. If someone has forced you to work and you are afraid to return to your home country you may be eligible for this protection. You would need to help law enforcement investigate the trafficking.

Driving While Undocumented

As you are likely aware, driving while undocumented is risky. If you are pulled over, you may be arrested. Some states allow police to turn people over to ICE after traffic stops. Others, like Illinois, do not. If you must drive, do so cautiously and be prepared for an encounter with police or ICE (see the Know Your Rights chapter).

If you can, get a driver's license. You will be driving legally and will be less likely to be arrested if you are pulled over.

States that allow undocumented immigrants to get a driver's license include California, Colorado, Connecticut, Delaware, District of Columbia, Hawaii, Illinois, Maryland, Nevada, New Jersey, New Mexico, New York, Oregon, Utah, Vermont, Virginia, and Washington.

Housing Protections

If you are undocumented, you may be worried about getting housing.

Federal laws. Regardless of your immigration status, the Federal Housing Act offers you some protections. Landlords or real estate agents cannot:

- Discriminate based on race, national origin, sex, religion, color, disability, or family status.
- Decide not to rent to you because you or your family members don't speak English.
- Refuse to rent to you because you are an immigrant from a particular country.
- Ask about your immigration status because of how you look, talk, or dress.

Landlords CAN ask about people's immigration status or citizenship, but if they do, they must ask all potential or existing tenants to provide information about their immigration status. That is, they can't single you out because of how you look or talk.

If you have been discriminated against, you can file a complaint with the Office of Fair Housing and Equal Opportunity. They do not ask about immigration status when people file a complaint. Call (800) 669-9777 (English and Spanish) to file a complaint.

Learn more here: https://www.hud.gov/program_offices/fair_housing_equal_opp/online-complaint

State laws. In some states like Illinois, Colorado, and California, landlords are not allowed to evict tenants on the basis of their citizenship or immigration status. They are also not allowed to disclose information about your status, contact ICE, or increase rent. The only time they may do so is when there is a court order or law is involved. If your landlord harasses you, threatens you, or retaliates against you, you can sue them in court.

Know Your Rights: ICE Encounters and the Removal Process

Knowing you might get deported is scary. But remember you have rights. This guide will help you understand these rights. This chapter can help you know what to do if you are stopped by the police or ICE. It will also help you know what to expect when the government tries to deport you. This can help you know when to get help and how to fight your case.

This chapter covers:

- ICE encounters: your legal rights
- The removal process, detention, and deportation: what to expect

ICE Encounters: Your Legal Rights

Deportation starts with an arrest. You may be arrested in one of the following ways:

- You are stopped and arrested by ICE.
- You are arrested by the police. The police then give your information to ICE.
- Are you in jail or prison? When you are released you may be arrested by ICE. It may depend on where you live.
- Maybe you've applied for immigration status. You are denied, and ICE arrests you.
- You are arrested at the border.

If you run into ICE or the police, it is very important you know your rights.

- You have the right to **remain silent.**
- You have the right to a **lawyer.**
- You have the right to **refuse to let ICE or an officer into your home.** But if they have a warrant you will have to let them in. A valid warrant is signed by a judge, NOT an immigration official. It has the address of the home and area to be searched.
- You have the right to **say no** if they want to search your body.
- You have the right to **refuse to sign anything** without help from a lawyer.
- You have the right to **refuse to show any documents** before talking with a lawyer.
- You have the right to a **hearing** to challenge your deportation order.

Print out a Know Your Rights red card. Here is one from the Immigration Legal Resource Center:

To print at home, use heavy weight paper, or card stock. Cut out the cards along the dotted lines. If you're unable to print on both sides, you can simply fold on the center line to make a 2-sided card.

If you use a professional printer, we suggest you print 2-sided cards with white text on red card stock with rounded corners.

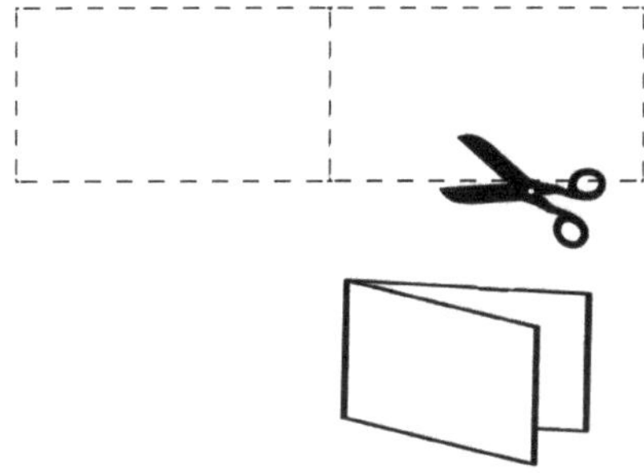

You have constitutional rights:

- DO NOT OPEN THE DOOR if an immigration agent is knocking on the door.
- DO NOT ANSWER ANY QUESTIONS from an immigration agent if they try to talk to you. You have the right to remain silent.
- DO NOT SIGN ANYTHING without first speaking to a lawyer. You have the right to speak with a lawyer.
- If you are outside of your home, ask the agent if you are free to leave and if they say yes, leave calmly.
- GIVE THIS CARD TO THE AGENT. If you are inside of your home, show the card through the window or slide it under the door.

I do not wish to speak with you, answer your questions, or sign or hand you any documents based on my 5th Amendment rights under the United States Constitution.

I do not give you permission to enter my home based on my 4th Amendment rights under the United States Constitution unless you have a warrant to enter, signed by a judge or magistrate with my name on it that you slide under the door.

I do not give you permission to search any of my belongings based on my 4th Amendment rights.

I choose to exercise my constitutional rights.

These cards are available to citizens and noncitizens alike.

You have constitutional rights:

- DO NOT OPEN THE DOOR if an immigration agent is knocking on the door.
- DO NOT ANSWER ANY QUESTIONS from an immigration agent if they try to talk to you. You have the right to remain silent.
- DO NOT SIGN ANYTHING without first speaking to a lawyer. You have the right to speak with a lawyer.
- If you are outside of your home, ask the agent if you are free to leave and if they say yes, leave calmly.
- GIVE THIS CARD TO THE AGENT. If you are inside of your home, show the card through the window or slide it under the door.

I do not wish to speak with you, answer your questions, or sign or hand you any documents based on my 5th Amendment rights under the United States Constitution.

I do not give you permission to enter my home based on my 4th Amendment rights under the United States Constitution unless you have a warrant to enter, signed by a judge or magistrate with my name on it that you slide under the door.

I do not give you permission to search any of my belongings based on my 4th Amendment rights.

I choose to exercise my constitutional rights.

These cards are available to citizens and noncitizens alike.

You have constitutional rights:

- DO NOT OPEN THE DOOR if an immigration agent is knocking on the door.
- DO NOT ANSWER ANY QUESTIONS from an immigration agent if they try to talk to you. You have the right to remain silent.
- DO NOT SIGN ANYTHING without first speaking to a lawyer. You have the right to speak with a lawyer.
- If you are outside of your home, ask the agent if you are free to leave and if they say yes, leave calmly.
- GIVE THIS CARD TO THE AGENT. If you are inside of your home, show the card through the window or slide it under the door.

I do not wish to speak with you, answer your questions, or sign or hand you any documents based on my 5th Amendment rights under the United States Constitution.

I do not give you permission to enter my home based on my 4th Amendment rights under the United States Constitution unless you have a warrant to enter, signed by a judge or magistrate with my name on it that you slide under the door.

I do not give you permission to search any of my belongings based on my 4th Amendment rights.

I choose to exercise my constitutional rights.

These cards are available to citizens and noncitizens alike.

You have constitutional rights:

- DO NOT OPEN THE DOOR if an immigration agent is knocking on the door.
- DO NOT ANSWER ANY QUESTIONS from an immigration agent if they try to talk to you. You have the right to remain silent.
- DO NOT SIGN ANYTHING without first speaking to a lawyer. You have the right to speak with a lawyer.
- If you are outside of your home, ask the agent if you are free to leave and if they say yes, leave calmly.
- GIVE THIS CARD TO THE AGENT. If you are inside of your home, show the card through the window or slide it under the door.

I do not wish to speak with you, answer your questions, or sign or hand you any documents based on my 5th Amendment rights under the United States Constitution.

I do not give you permission to enter my home based on my 4th Amendment rights under the United States Constitution unless you have a warrant to enter, signed by a judge or magistrate with my name on it that you slide under the door.

I do not give you permission to search any of my belongings based on my 4th Amendment rights.

I choose to exercise my constitutional rights.

These cards are available to citizens and noncitizens alike.

There are some things you should and shouldn't do if you run into ICE. Practice answering ICE questions with your family and friends.

Do

- Stay calm.
- Say "I am choosing to exercise my legal right to remain silent," or give them a "know your rights" card (see above).
- Call a lawyer right away. Ask for a list of free or low-cost legal options if you don't have one. See the Know Your Rights chapter for more information about ways to fight your case.
- Carry your valid work permit or green card with you all the time.
- Ask for an interpreter.
- Ask them to show you their badge, identification, or warrant.
- Are you worried about arrest? Let the officer know you have children. People with kids are often allowed to stay with their families instead of being arrested.
- Record everything on a phone or camera, if you can.
- Take notes of everything that happens. Note the officer's badge number, who they work for, and name.

Don't

- Run, argue, or resist.
- Open your door unless they show you a warrant.
- Answer any questions.
- Sign anything without advice from a lawyer.
- Carry any documents about your country of origin.
- Lie or give fake documents.
- Share any information about your immigration status, where you were born, or how you came to the US.

The Removal Process, Detention, and Deportation: What to Expect

What does the removal process look like?

Lots of things can happen when you get arrested. There is no single way that the removal process will happen. Please see the chart below for the most common processes after arrest. Fortunately, there are many spots during the process where you can get help and fight your case.

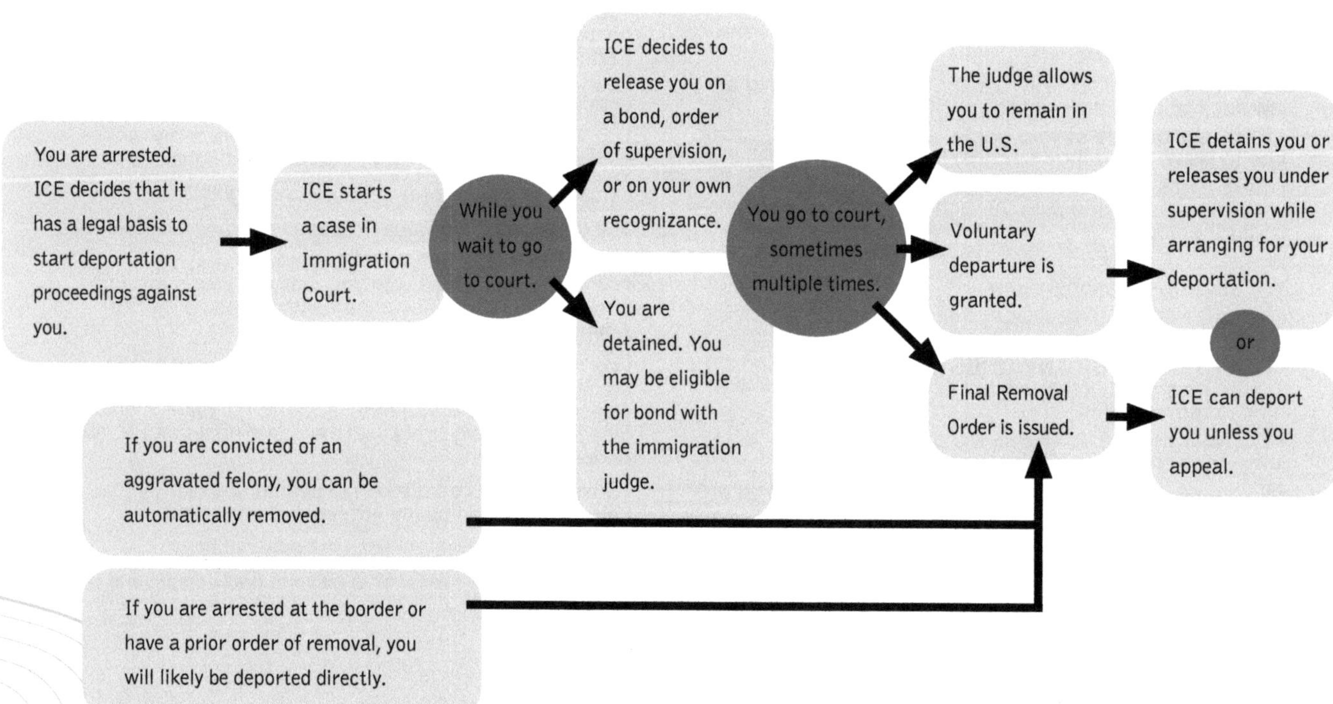

KNOW YOUR RIGHTS:

WHAT TO DO IF IMMIGRATION OR THE POLICE COME TO YOUR DOOR

STOP AND THINK TWICE WHEN SOMEONE COMES TO YOUR DOOR

You're not normally required to open the door to anyone. Immigration and the police can't come into your home without a warrant signed by a judge.

REMAIN SILENT

You have the right to remain silent.
Immigration can use anything you say against you.

STAY CALM AND DO NOT RUN

Use your phone to take photos and notes about the raid, but stay calm and do not run.

ASK TO SPEAK TO YOUR ATTORNEY AND THINK TWICE BEFORE SIGNING ANYTHING

Do not sign forms you don't understand or don't want to sign. A lawyer who knows deportation defense may be able to help you fight your case.

*This information is not intended as legal advice.

iAmerica has a list of legal services if you need a lawyer.
Visit iAmerica at: iAmerica.org/LegalHelp

You may encounter the following agencies in this process:

- Department of Homeland Security
    - Immigration and Customs Enforcement (ICE),
    - Customs and Border Protection (CBP),
    - U.S. Citizenship and Immigration Services (USCIS)
- Department of Justice (Executive Office of Immigration Review (EOIR))
- Department of Health and Human Services (detention of unaccompanied minors)

Will I go to court or be deported directly?
It depends on your situation. If you are afraid to return to your home country, you should tell an immigration official. You will then be referred to an asylum officer for a credible or reasonable fear interview. You'll also be deported right away if you already have an order of removal. If you have been ordered removed before, it is important to speak to an immigration attorney to see if there is anything else that can be done.

You have the right to see an immigration judge. ICE will serve you with a document called a "Notice to Appear." This document will tell you the charges that the government of the United States is alleging against you. Depending on your particular facts you may be eligible for a way to remain in the United States even though proceedings have been initiated against you.

There are ways you can stay in the US, for example if you claim asylum. This means you are in danger if you go back to your country. If ICE decides to take you to court you will talk to an immigration agent. The agent will tell you the charges against you and set a court date. You will get a Notice to Appear (NTA) before the court or an appointment for Deferred Inspection.

Will I be detained?
Maybe. The law lets the government detain you while they decide your case. Whether you are detained or not depends on a lot of things. Some of the factors that the immigration judge may take into account are whether you've been convicted of a felony or whether you have young kids. Some states and cities cooperate with ICE, and ICE is able to detain lots of people. Other states and cities do not cooperate with ICE, and it is possible that you will avoid being picked up by ICE.

If I am in prison or jail, will I be deported after release?
It depends. In some states, ICE works with prisons and jails. They detain and deport people after they leave prison. In other states, you may be released. But ICE may arrest you later. ICE can issue a "Final Administrative Order of Removal." If you are not offered a hearing, contact an immigration lawyer or immigrant advocacy organization to be connected to one.

What if I'm afraid of going back to my home country?
If you are scared to go back you may be able to stay. You can file an asylum claim. Read our chapter Getting Help to Fight Your Case for more information. If you already have a removal order or are given one when detained by ICE, you will need to act very quickly. Tell ICE you are afraid to return to your home country and look for a lawyer.

Where will I be detained?

You will be processed at an ICE processing facility, holding facility, or a field office. If ICE decides to keep you in custody, you will go to a private detention center, county jail, or ICE-run facility. You may be detained in a different state.

Your family can look up where you are here: https://locator.ice.gov/odls/

To find you they will need:

- Your Alien Registration Number (A-Number) and country of birth. ICE gives you an A-Number during your detention. If you have had contact with immigration before, you should have one already.
- If they don't know your Alien Registration Number, they can also search by name, country of birth, and date of birth.

A list of detention facilities, their addresses, and phone numbers can be found at https://www.ice.gov/detention-facilities.

How long will I be detained?

It depends. If you are waiting for court, you may have to wait a few weeks. If you are waiting for deportation, you may wait a few days or a few months. It depends how fast the government can get papers for you from your home country.

If I am detained, can I ask for a release?

ICE has the discretion to release you on your own recognizance. If a bond is set, you can pay the bond and leave.

If I am released, will I be supervised?

It depends. ICE may issue an ankle monitor if it releases you under an order of supervision. Immigration judges can only issue bonds; they can't issue ankle monitors. You may have to check in with ICE periodically.

Can I have a lawyer represent me at immigration court?

Yes. You have a right to use a lawyer. The court does not give one to most people in immigration court. See the directory or visit https://www.immigrationadvocates.org/nonprofit/legaldirectory/ or https://www.justice.gov/eoir/list-pro-bono-legal-service-providers for a list of organizations that can help with immigration and free lawyers.

Can my family members visit me and bring me things while in detention?

Yes, usually. They can usually bring you a small bag of clothes (up to 40 pounds), toiletries (but no liquids), and money (US dollars or your home country's currency). These things will make your deportation much easier because:

- You will not look like a deportee at the border.
- You will have money for transportation, food and other things at the border.
- You may even be able to help others who are being deported with you.

With the pandemic some facilities have not been letting people bring in items. Have your family or friends check before they bring you a bag.

What is it like in detention?

Detention can look very different, depending on where you are. Below we share a few people's experience with detention.

Be sure that the person that brings your things isn't undocumented. It's a detention center and it's possible that they may be asked about their migration status.

—Roberto L.

Deportation is very stressful. You get moved around a lot at all hours of the night. But once you get to your final destination things get better. You'll be with people from all parts of Mexico. You may even be able to make friends who live near you. They can help you plan your trip from the border to your hometown so you won't travel on your own. When you get to ICE you will not have anything, but your countrymen will gladly share what they have until you can get your hands on some things yourself.

—Erick N.

Unfortunately, immigration detention can be very difficult for some people, especially those who stay in custody for a longer period of time and/or have medical or mental health issues.

> *Even though immigration detention is not supposed to be a form of punishment, it can feel that way. People are subject to the same rules and conditions as those in criminal custody, such as lockdowns and being sent to solitary confinement. A lot of the time we hear from clients that they are not getting medication they need or are not able to see a doctor when they need to, that the jail is dirty, or that they are being treated badly by guards. This is not okay, and you should report these problems right away.*
>
> **– Immigration attorney, Chicago, IL**

How can I report detention issues?

If you have a lawyer, make sure to let them know so that they can try to help. In addition, you can make reports to DHS and to immigration advocates at Freedom for Immigrants:

- DHS Office of the Inspector General. (800) 323-8603
- ICE ERO Detention Reporting and Information Line. (888) 351-4024 or https://www.ice.gov/webform/ero-contact-form
- ICE Office of Professional Responsibility (Joint Intake Center). (877) 246-8253, or by email at joint.intake@dhs.gov
- Freedom for Immigrants Hotline from any facility phone: 9233# or have a friend or family member call their Family Support Line at (209) 757-3733

Your country's consulate may be able to help you. You should not contact them if you are asking for asylum, since claiming asylum means that you are saying that your country is unable to protect you.

What should I do if I am sexually assaulted or abused while in detention?

Sadly, sexual assault and abuse does happen in detention facilities. However, there are laws that require facilities to investigate sexual abuse. In addition to reporting the abuse to the detention facility, there are a couple of other ways you, your attorney, or family members can report sexual abuse. You can also report neglect or any retaliation you experience for reporting abuse. Reports are confidential and can be made anonymously, both verbally and in writing, to the offices listed above.

Plan for Possible Deportation

You can prepare for arrest and deportation.

This chapter covers:

- Gather important documents
- Gather important phone numbers
- Create a family plan for children
- Save money

Gather Important Documents

Gather your important documents and keep them in a safe place. They can help if you are detained. They will also help you build a life in your home country if you are deported. You can also share them with a lawyer or an adult caregiver in case of emergency.

These documents will help you prepare for possible deportation.

Document or number	Description, how to get it
Alien Registration Number (A Number). The letter A followed by 8 or 9 numbers.	If you have applied for a green card, you should have an Alien Registration Number. This is the number that ICE will use to identify you during removal proceedings. Your loved ones can use this number to find where you are. Your A Number can be found on a Work Permit, Green Card, Immigrant Visa, or Immigrant Fee Handout, Notice of Action or other items.
CURP code, a unique identity code for citizens and residents of Mexico.	Look up your CURP number online at www.consultas.curp.gob.mx.
RFC, a unique registration number issued by the SAT (Mexican tax authority).	Find your RFC. If you have your CURP you can look up your RFC here: https://www54.sat.gob.mx/curp/Consult
Birth certificates (your own or your children's)	To get a copy of your birth certificate from Mexico, write to or call the Mexican consulate in your area (see address in the directory). You can also get it online at https://www.gob.mx/ActaNacimiento/ For children born in the US, get their birth certificate from the county clerk in the county where they were born.
Immigration documents (work permit, green card, visa, etc.) or documents demonstrating your residence in the U.S.	Gather any kind of immigration documents that you or your family members have.

Social Security cards or Individual Taxpayer Identification Numbers (ITIN) for yourself or any family members	To get a lost ITIN, call the IRS ITIN Hotline at (800) 908-9982. To ask for a replacement US Social Security card, go to https://www.ssa.gov/myaccount/replacement-card.html. You can also call (800) 772-1213.
Marriage license	If you were married in the US, you can get a marriage certificate or divorce decree from the county clerk's office where you were married or divorced. If you got married in Mexico you will need to contact the Civil Registry in the county where you were married.
Passport	Are you eligible for a US passport? Find more information about the process here: https://travel.state.gov/content/travel/en/passports.html/ If you need your Mexican passport, you can make an appointment with your local consulate. It's a good idea to get passports for your kids so they can come see you.
Military discharge papers	Contact the branch of the armed services where you served.
Driver's license	Contact your local Department of Motor Vehicles. If you can get a US license, get it. If it's expired, get it renewed if possible. US driver's licenses are accepted in Mexico.
US bank account information	This can be found on monthly statements. It can also be found on the information you were given when you opened your account. You can also download it from the bank's website if you have online banking.
Health records	Collect your health records from your doctor and all of your family's. Write down insurance information, a medication list, and doctor's contact information.
Education records, for yourself and your children	Gather any school records or transcripts. These will need to be notarized to be recognized in Mexico (see the Apostille process below).
Car records	Car titles, license plate #, VIN/ID #, car loan, insurance
Financial records	Bank account information, numbers to call.
Apartment rental or home ownership, mortgage documents	Make a copy of your lease. If you own a home, make a copy of the mortgage and ownership documents.
Government assistance documents	If you or your family members qualify for programs such as TANF, Link, WIC, or Medicaid, keep copies of these documents in the folder.

Apostille Process

You have all your important US documents. Now how do you use them in Mexico, or other countries? You'll need to go through a process of getting an "apostille." An apostille is a document that will let you use your documents in your home country. To complete the apostille process, you'll need to first get the document notarized by a notary public.

You should start the apostille process while you are still in the United States. Once you notarize everything, mail your documents to a Secretary of State's office (see below). Ask them for the apostille. The cost depends on the state. In Illinois it's just $2. The process usually takes five to seven days. You can usually do it by mail or in person.

Search online for "apostille" and the name of your state. This can help you find instructions on the apostille process. You can have a family member or friend help you. You can also hire a lawyer to do it for you. Learn more at www.apostille.net.

See the directory for apostille process locations (Secretary of State offices) in various states.

If your transcript is sent directly to your employer from your college or university you may not have to go through the apostille process. In general employers and institutions will accept documents that come directly from US institutions.

—Roberto L.

Documents that you can gather after deportation include your ID (called INE in Mexico), CURP, RFC if you don't have them currently, your passport and driver's license. Learn more in the chapter Getting Your IDs and Documents.

Shipping documents to Mexico

Getting documents sent to Mexico or your home country is expensive. It takes a long time. You might want to send copies to a family member or friend in your home country now. The Mexican postal service can be unreliable. Send important documents by FedEx, DHL, or UPS. You can also scan your documents and save them. Family members can email them to you.

Gather Important Phone Numbers

If you are at risk for deportation, gather the following important phone numbers

	Name of contact	Phone number
Insurance companies (health, car, home)		
Immigration nonprofit organization		
Consulate of your home country		
Lawyer/legal service providers		
Church contacts		
Emergency caregiver for children		
Family emergency contacts–in US		

Family emergency contacts–in home country		
Schools where children attend		
Doctors, therapists and counselors		
Dentists		
Employer or union rep.		
People who can (or cannot) pick up your children from school/daycare		
Bank		

Create a Family Plan

Do you have young kids? Do you take care of other relatives? You are probably worried about what will happen to them if you are detained or deported.

One thing you can do is create a family plan. A family plan will help you prepare. It will help you arrange for your children's care and education. It will make things easier for them if you are deported.

Below are some things you should have in your family plan.

Decide who will take care of your children if you are detained or deported. Find an adult you trust and who your children know. Talk to them. Talk about what will happen if you are arrested, detained, or deported. Let their caregiver know you are listing them as an emergency contact.

Update emergency contact information at your child's school. Memorize their phone numbers.

Talk to your children about your plan. If your children are old enough, make sure that they have contact information for their caregiver. Give them contact information for friends and family in your home country who they can call to get in touch with you.

Legal Documents. There are some documents that can help your caregiver take care of your kids. Here are a few options:

Caregiver Authorization Affidavit. This form lets your caregiver take care of your kids. The caregiver can send them to school and take them to the doctor.

Power of Attorney. This form gives a caregiver power to make most decisions that a parent would make for their child.

Legal Guardianship. This option is more permanent. It would mean you have less rights to make decisions about your kids. Ask a lawyer if you decide to let someone else be your children's legal guardian.

Emancipation Petition. Are your children 16 or 17? Are they mature enough to manage things on their own? Consider an emancipation petition. This would let them stay in the states without you.

See the Legal Matters chapter for more information on how to find a lawyer.

Documents for Your Child's Caregiver. Create an important documents folder for your child's caregiver. It should include the following:

Document or resource	Description	Taken care of?
Caregiver authorization documents	Caregiver Affidavit, Power of Attorney, Legal Guardianship	
Emergency contact information	Babysitter, doctor, school, attorney, family and friends in your home country	
Copies of identification documents	Birth certificates, social security cards	
Medical information	Insurance cards, vaccination records, dental records, doctor phone numbers, health records	
School info and records	Phone numbers of school, teachers, report cards, transcripts.	
Money to care for your child, if possible	Think about what kind of expenses they may have.	

☆ Do you have a family pet? Decide who will take care of it. Be sure to give them information about the pet's health needs and vet contact.

These websites have more info about how to create a family plan.

- https://www.ilrc.org/family-preparedness-plan
- https://www.informedimmigrant.com/guides/steps-take-prepare-family/

Save Money

If you can, it's a good idea to save some money. Detention and deportation can be expensive.

Save money for:

- Legal fees
- Travel expenses
- Childcare expenses
- Funds to use in your home country while you find a job

Getting Help to Fight Your Case

Do you want to fight your case in court? We recommend you reach out for help.

This chapter covers the following:
- Legal help
- Help from your home country
- Applying for asylum or other protections

Legal Help

Get legal help with your case. Immigration court won't often provide a lawyer for you, but you have the right to one. In some places, such as Chicago and New York, there are programs where non-profits and public defender offices provide free representation to people appearing before the immigration court. Requirements to participate vary but check to see if there is a program in your area.

A lawyer can help you through the challenges of the legal system. You can represent yourself, but lawyers understand the rules better. You can get low-cost or free (pro bono) legal help in the US.

Find low-cost or pro bono (free) legal services here:

- https://www.immigrationlawhelp.org/
- https://www.immigrationadvocates.org/nonprofit/legaldirectory/
- https://www.uscis.gov/avoid-scams/find-legal-services
- https://ailalawyer.com
- https://www.justice.gov/eoir/list-pro-bono-legal-service-providers
- https://unitedwedream.org/our-work/deportation-defense/
- https://immigrantsrising.org/legalintake/

To learn more about your rights and what you should do when you run into ICE or police, check out these resources:

- https://www.aclu.org/know-your-rights/immigrants-rights/
- https://www.informedimmigrant.com/guides/know-your-rights/
- https://iamerica.org/know-your-rights
- https://www.illinoislegalaid.org/legal-information/fighting-deportation-or-removal-case

Help From Your Home Country

Your country's consulate may be able to help you. Contact them as soon as you are arrested or detained. They can give you consular help and help to protect your interests. See our Directory for a list of consulates in the US.

The Mexican government runs a program called "Héroes Paisanos." It protects the rights of Mexican citizens as they enter, travel through, and leave the country. They publish a guide that's useful for planning your return to Mexico. Scan the QR code below or click this link. https://www.gob.mx/cms/uploads/attachment/file/714447/GUIA_PAISANO_2022_COMPLETA.pdf

Applying for Asylum and Other Protections

What is asylum?

Are you afraid of harm or persecution in your home country? Asylum lets people stay in the US instead of being deported if they have those fears. If you are not eligible for asylum you may be eligible for withholding of removal or protection under the Convention Against Torture. All are covered under the same application. Here's a great source of information on applying for protection: http://www.firrp.org/media/Asylum_WOR_CAT-Guide-2013.pdf

Who is eligible to apply?

You must be in the US or trying to get into the US at a port of entry. You must apply within one year of getting to the US, no matter your immigration status. You are barred from asylum if you have been convicted of an aggravated felony. https://www.uscis.gov/humanitarian/refugees-and-asylum/asylum/asylum-frequently-asked-questions/questions-and-answers-asylum-eligibility-and-applications

How do I apply for protection?

Complete Form I-589, Application for Asylum and for Withholding of Removal: https://www.uscis.gov/i-589. This form lets you apply for asylum for you. In some circumstances you may include your family and children if they are under 21 years old, unmarried and in the U.S.

How long will I have to wait?

Decisions about asylum are generally made at the end of the hearing and you are notified right away. Sometimes it may take longer.

Preparing for Life in Your Home Country

Reach Out to Friends and Family

Do you worry about getting deported? If so, try to reach out to people who can support you. Who are the people you're counting on to be there for you?

Contact family members and friends in the United States and your home country. Be honest about what you need from them. Let them know if you need housing, money, advice or support. Find out what they expect from you.

Deportation can be very lonely. Please know that others are going through this too.

☆ Do you live in Mexico City? There are a couple of organizations that can help you. Otros Dreams in Acción (www.odamexico.org) is one. See the chapter Voting and Engaging with Your Community and the directory for the contact information of organizations that can help.

> *You choose how you want to live. Stay positive and accept the deportation happened so you can move on.*
> **—Julia B.**

Assess Your Finances

Save as much money as you can. If you don't have a lot of money, ask family or friends to send you some while you wait to be deported. Have them bring you the currency of your country. That way you don't have to worry about exchanging money right after your deportation.

Think about how you will get money after deportation. Will someone lend you money in Mexico or your home country? Will you rely on wire transfers from loved ones in the US?

Charles Schwab is a US bank that does not charge ATM fees in Mexico. Open an account and ask for two debit cards. Keep one for yourself and give one to a loved one in the US. Your loved one can put money in the account. Then, you can withdraw it for free in Mexico. This way you won't have to rely on wire transfers.

Health

If you can, get a dental exam, an eye exam, and a physical exam. This can help you deal with any health concerns. Start by searching for local free and low-cost health clinics in your area.

Next, get your medications ready. If you take prescription medication, get at least a 30-day supply. You can take them with you if you are detained and deported.

Finally, plan to apply for government or private health insurance in your home country. See the Health chapter to learn more.

Learn About the Culture of Your Home Country

Learn as much as you can about the culture of your home country. Read and watch the news. Pick up a history book or even a novel from your culture. All of this will help you adjust better.

You may have culture shock when you get there. Things may have changed a lot. Life may be very different from the US. For example, things move a lot slower in Mexico due to the bureaucracy. See the section on Cultural Encounters to get an idea of what to expect.

> *When I got here I couldn't get a job because I wasn't fluent in Spanish, I wasn't up to date with current events, with the culture. Study up on the history, culture, politics. You need to know all that to move around and not stick out like a sore thumb.*
>
> **—Israel G.**

Preparing for Your Job Search

You may be worried about finding a job in your home country. Below we describe some ways you can prepare for your job search.

Consider Pay

It's good to know what fair pay is in different parts of the country. At the border in Ciudad Juárez you can find work in a factory for 260 pesos a day (about $13 USD). In other parts of the country and in other industries, you will be paid by the hour. For example, an English teacher in Morelia, Michoacán may make 75-90 pesos an hour ($3-4 USD) working in a public school. In larger cities wages are a little higher (100 or 120 pesos an hour, depending on the job).

Minimum Wage in Mexico		
	Minimum wage per day (2023)	**US dollars (at the time of publication)**
In most of the country	207 pesos	$11.50
In the Northern Border Zone	312 pesos	$17

☆ Do you have a felony conviction? We have some good news. If you live in Southern Mexico, most employers do not run a background check. If you are near the border and applying to US companies, expect background checks.

> *Once you move to Mexico, be realistic. 100 pesos is like $5 dollars, in the US that's cheap! In Mexico that's the minimum wage!*
>
> **—Julia B.**

Build Experience

There are some things you can do in the US to make your job search easier:

- Get an education. Get your GED, Adult Basic Education, or go to college.
- Gain work experience.
- Gain skills.
- Volunteer. This can help you gain skills and can go on your resume.
- Learn English or Spanish. Take a class, talk to native speakers and read in English. If your Spanish is rusty, do all you can to improve it while you are in the US.
- Write or update your resume or "curriculúm" in Spanish. There are some differences between what should be included on a resume in the US and in Mexico. See the Employment chapter for more information. There are sample resumes in the back of this guide as well.

Be ready to pivot. Be patient with yourself. You're eager to ... do all of those things. Be realistic with yourself, what you can really do, what is within your control. You're going to be facing a lot of things.

—Roberto L.

Networking

What might you do for work in your home country? Talk with family and friends. They can help you get information, connect with new people, and find jobs. If you have a resume, send it to friends and family members. Ask them to share it with employers. See the Employment section to learn more.

Think about the skills you have as someone who has lived in the US. English skills will take you far. So will a cultural understanding of the US. The Mexican government has a program to fill many English teaching positions. These jobs have good salaries and benefits. Learn more in the Employment chapter.

Be hopeful. Many people have found jobs after deportation. With the right preparation and attitude, you can, too.

Moving Your Family

For some families, the decision to move is easy. For others it requires a lot of thought. You may be worried about how it will affect your family. Your children will be changing schools and your partner will have to find friends and work. No matter what, deportation is hard. If your family comes with you they may have a hard time in your home country. If they stay behind they will have to deal with missing you. Both situations are very hard on families.

The decision to move your family is personal. There is no right answer. It depends a lot on your situation. If you think you can get back to the US quickly, it may not be worth the move. But if you will call your new country home, a move may be best.

Many people who have made the move to Mexico say they wish they had spoken more Spanish at home. Speaking more Spanish can help prepare children for school. Sadly, children who don't speak Spanish get bullied in Mexican schools. Think about enrolling your children in any Spanish class at school. You can also enroll them in an after-school program to learn Spanish. Make speaking Spanish at home fun. Play games with the kids in Spanish, label items in the house with their Spanish name, or watch children's TV shows in Spanish.

For information on getting your family's documents ready for the move, see the Make a Plan chapter.

> *"Moving is not easy but if it's what's best for your family, it's worth it to rebuild a life together that's yours."*
> **—Katerina B.**

Changing Relationships

Be aware that your relationships with your family may change after you move to your home country. Maybe you used to send money home to support relatives. But now you may be the one that needs help. This can be tough. Some deported families have said they sent money home for years. But they did not feel welcome when returning home. Think ahead about this and how it will affect your family.

Be prepared for shifting roles with your partner and kids. Maybe your partner didn't work in the US. But now you need more money, so they have to work. If your partner is a US citizen they may even be able to make a lot more money than you. Be open to change. Your new life is different. You will need to get used to it. But you can use these changes to grow and reflect.

> *Know that at the end of the day everything will be okay.*
> **—Missy L.**

At the Border

☆ If you are from Guatemala, Honduras or El Salvador, please see the section on deportation to Central America.

If you are being deported to Mexico, you will either take a bus or a plane to the border. If you take a plane, it may make other stops. It depends on where you are being deported from. If you are deported from Chicago, you will probably make stops in the south. But if you are in Georgia, you might be the last stop of a plane coming from the north. Once the plane lands, you will be put on a bus. The bus will take you to the border. Officers will open a large gate and tell you to cross the bridge.

Most of the time you will find Mexican immigration officials to help you. Read on for more information about Grupos Beta and other Mexican government assistance.

It is important to think about what you will do after you get to the border. Will you stay in a shelter nearby? Will you take a bus to your home? Will someone be meeting you? A meeting might be hard to arrange. You will not know your drop-off location until you get there. ICE keeps this information from you so you don't try to plan your return illegally.

Where Will You be Deported To?

What border city you will be deported from depends on where you live in the US. For example, people from Illinois have been released in Matamoros, Tamaulipas, at the border with Brownsville, TX, as well as the Reynosa/ McAllen, TX border crossing. Contact your local Mexican consulate to find out where you might be dropped.

Some ICE offices can deport people straight to Mexico City. Check with your local consulate to see if you can do this.

Grupos Beta (Beta Program)

On the other side, you will likely find Mexican immigration officials to help you. The Mexican government offers a program for people returning to Mexico called the Beta Program (Grupos Beta). They will give you water and a small meal. They can also get you a temporary ID and transportation information. Sometimes they can give you a ride to a place to change money or to the bus station, with a discounted ticket. They will let you make phone calls and use the internet wherever you arrive.

They also offer a warning. They often tell people not to stay in the border area, especially after dark. They will tell you that crime is high there. For your safety, you should plan on taking the next bus south. If you don't plan to take a bus, they may offer to take you to a nearby shelter. People from states with high cartel activity (Michoacán, Sinaloa) should especially leave the area quickly. Try not to tell anyone where you are from.

> Because of COVID-19, the Mexican government has hired buses to take you out of the border states. Follow government officials' instructions at the border to stay safe.

> *At the border stick together, help each other.*
>
> **—Ramon C.**

Be super patient during the deportation process. There's a lot of waiting, sitting around, and you won't know what's happening next. Prepare yourself mentally for this. There is a lot of uncertainty.

—Ramon C.

Stay hydrated. I remember being really thirsty once we hit the road so manage your water intake and go to the bathroom every chance you get because you don't know when you will get the chance again.

—Ramon C.

Be patient. Stay positive. Eventually they will take you to a safe place.

—Alex A.

Once at the border, Mexican immigration will give you food and a temporary ID and will urge you to get to the bus terminal as soon as possible. They also give rides to the terminal so just wait until they take you. Once at the terminal, you will need to buy a ticket. If you live deep in Mexico, like Michoacán as I did, there will NOT be direct buses there. You will have to take a bus to other nearby cities to pick other people up or to get a different bus altogether so calculate enough money to take multiple buses depending on how far south you are going. Bus tickets range from around $10 USD (200 pesos) to around $100 USD (2,000 pesos) depending, of course, on where you are going.

—Erick N.

Deportation to Mexico City

You may be able to take a flight right to Mexico City. But not all deported people can do this. Check with your local Mexican consulate to see if you qualify to fly to Mexico City.

There are not as many flights to Mexico City as there used to be. There are also not as many government programs to help people deported to the capital. Some non-governmental organizations help returning citizens. Otros Dreams en Acción is one, and Deportados Unidos en la Lucha in neighboring Estado de México is another. See directory for more information on those organizations.

You've got to have people to help you. Make contact with people in your home country and try to have someone waiting for you when you get there.

—Israel G.

In case you are deported to an area where there is no Beta Group, stick together. Stay in well-lit areas and be aware that people will pick up on the fact that you are not from here and may try to take advantage of you. Don't talk to anyone you don't need to and keep an eye on your bag.

—Ramon C.

Worksheet

It may be hard to think about deportation. It's ok to feel nervous or scared. Use those feelings to motivate yourself to plan. Don't let it overwhelm you and stop you from acting.

1. Make a guess about what border city you might be deported to. You'll probably be deported to a city that is closest to where you live in the US. For instance, people in Illinois could be deported to Brownsville because it is south of Illinois. They probably won't be deported to Tijuana, which is far away from Illinois. Check with your local Mexican consulate to see where you can expect to be deported. What are **two cities** you might be deported to?

2. Do you know anyone in these places that might be able to meet you? Ask friends and family and others that you are incarcerated or detained with. Write their names, location and phone numbers below.

Name	City	Phone Number

3. What will you do when you arrive at the border?
    a. Someone I know will meet me.
    b. Get on a bus to my final destination where I have family or friends.
    c. Stay at a shelter at the border. See our Directory for possible locations.

Planning to Return to the US?

Many people say they planned to return illegally right away. They didn't plan for life in Mexico because they planned to cross back. They caution you NOT to do this. Here's why:

First, the border region is very dangerous. It would be dangerous to stay there while you planned your reentry. There have been reports of kidnapping and people being forced to join organized crime organizations.

Second, if you get caught you could pay fines or go to prison. People who enter illegally after deportation can be fined and/or imprisoned for up to two years. But if you have a felony conviction it is even worse. People caught reentering who have a felony conviction can be imprisoned for up to 20 years (Reentry of removed aliens 8 U.S.C.A. 1326).

I was desperate to go back. I never wanted to live here. And the whole first year I was resisting the idea of making a life here. That attitude made it harder for me to adjust. But once I accepted living here, I put all my efforts into getting ahead here. Learning the language, making contacts and getting focused on living here. If you give it your all, if you are committed to living here you can actually make a good living and have a happy life here. I'm here, I'm working, I'm living and I'm happy.

—Israel G.

Center for Information and Assistance for Mexicans (CIAM)

All the information you need is just one call away!

What's the CIAM?

CIAM is a call center that brings you comprehensive counseling on subjects such as:

·Consular services
·Current immigration policy
·Prevention and consular protection

What does CIAM do for you?

· **Assists** you in locating family and friends.
· **Advises** you on both legal and immigration matters.
· **Informs** you about current immigration policy.
· **Counsels** you if you've been the victim of abuse or fraud.

w to interact with immigration authorit

1. Have an **emergency plan**:
Protect your family, especially children. If your kids were born in the United States, go to your nearest consulate to register them as Mexicans.

2. Find out which **documents should be kept with you at all times**.
Keep them in a safe place.

e information, contact the nearest
te of Mexico or the **CIAM**.

t give ICE the right to enter your

3. If you need information abo
immigration, head to your nea
consulate. They can point you
attorneys

4. Know your rights at home,
and in public.

If immigration authorities come to

- Do not open the door.
- Stay calm.
- Do not run away.
- Do not provide your immigrat
- Ask them to show you the wa
through the window. Check if t
has your name, address and the
signature.
- If they do not have a warrant, y
the right to refuse to let them in

thorities **arrest you**:

silent.
eveal your immigration status.
to speak to your consulate.
to speak to your attorney.
ign anything.
which agency arrested you
al police department, ICE,
rol, etc).
an interpreter and a bail.
e.
how fake documents.

5. If authorities enter your home **without a warrant**:

- Ask respectfully for their names and say "I do not consent to the search".

Part 2: Life After Deportation

- Getting your IDs and Documents
- Resources to Meet Basic Needs
- Employment
- Education
- Health
- Communications
- Legal Matters
- Finances, Credit, and Taxes
- Voting and Engaging with Your Community
- Cultural Encounters

Getting Your IDs and Documents

One of the first things you should do in your home country is to gather your documents and get a permanent ID. If you are deported to Mexico, you will get a temporary ID. The temporary ID is official, but you will need to get an INE soon. An INE is the most common official form of ID in Mexico. You need an ID to open a bank account, get housing, get a job, and apply for health care and educational programs.

☆ The organization Documenta has a website with links you can follow to get your ID and documents. They also have great information on jobs, mental health, social services, and education. https://restart.documenta.org.mx/

Birth Certificate

If you do not have a copy of your birth certificate, get one as soon as possible. You need a birth certificate to get an INE. You can use an old copy of your birth certificate to get your INE. But you should also get a certified birth certificate. You'll need it for things like getting a marriage license.

How to Request Your Birth Certificate

There are two ways to get your birth certificate:

- In person at the Civil Registry (Régistro Civil) in the place where you were born. It is usually part of the town hall- ayuntamiento or alcaldía. See the directory at the back of this guide for the one closest to you, or consult their website: https://embamex.sre.gob.mx/argentina/images/consular/ofregcivilenrepubmexic. The Civil Registry also does marriage, divorce, and death certificates.
- Online at https://www.gob.mx/ActaNacimiento/. To get it online you will need your CURP (Clave Única de Registro de Población or Unique Population Registry Code)

You will be asked for your:

- Complete name
- Sex
- CURP (see below)
- Complete names of your parents
- Date and place where your birth was originally registered

The fee for your birth certificate is different for every state. It will be between around 60 to 220 pesos. You can check the exact cost here: https://www.gob.mx/tramites/ficha/expedicion-de-la-copia-certificada-del-acta-de-nacimiento-en-linea/RENAPO187

INE

"INE," pronounced "Eee-Nay," is your official ID. It is like a state ID or driver's license in the US. INE stands for "Instituto Nacional Electoral" or National Electoral Institute. With your INE you can vote in all elections. It is a national ID, not a state ID like in the US. The INE is the most commonly accepted form of ID in Mexico. There is no charge for getting an INE.

How to Request Your INE

Make an appointment at your local Civil Registry office or go to the nearest "Módulo de atención ciudadana" (citizen attention module). See the directory in the back of this guide or search the most current information on https://ubicatumodulo.ine.mx/. You can also make an appointment online here: https://app-inter.ife.org.mx/siac2011/citas_initCapturaCitas.siac. You can go without an appointment but it might take longer.

You might be getting it for the first time. Or maybe you just need a replacement or to change your address. There are different ways to ask for your INE.

To get an INE for the first time, you will need to bring with you:

- Photo ID: A military, state, or professional ID, NOT your temporary ID. If you do not have a photo ID, you can bring two witnesses with you who live in the same town as you. They will need to bring their original, current INEs.
- Proof of address document (no more than 3 months old): electricity (CFE), telephone bill, water or property tax bill. If you have no proof of address in your own name, you can ask your witnesses to bring their own proof of address document.

Even if you don't have all your documents ready, make the appointment. It could be a month or more before you can get an appointment and it can take up to six months to get your INE. If you need to reschedule your appointment, do it as soon as possible.
—Roberto L.

If you need two witnesses to prove identity but don't know anyone, contact a local organization that assists migrants. In Guadalajara, the Rhizome Center for Migrants offers this service (+52 33 2182 0836)

It will take about 7-15 days for your INE to be ready. They will give you a document that proves you asked for your the INE as well as the date of pick up. Pick up the ID at the same place where you requested it. Bring the document they gave you, sign your name, and be fingerprinted to receive your INE. You can check the status of your INE application here: https://consulta-tramite.ine.mx/nacional/archivos2/portal/credencial/tramite/.

If you have requested an INE and you didn't get it on time or your application was denied, you can submit a legal complaint here: https://portalanterior.ine.mx/archivos3/portal/historico/recursos/IFE-v2/DERFE/DERFE-FormatosTramites/Sol_DDPE.pdf.

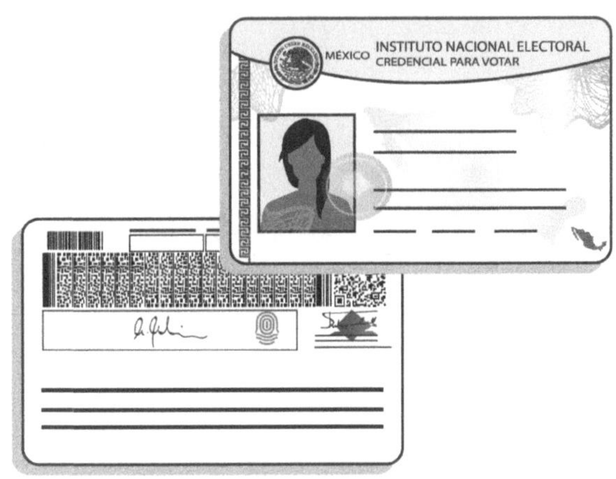

CURP (La Clave Única de Registro de Población)

The CURP is like a Social Security number in the US. It is a number that identifies you as you. You need it to do many things in Mexico, such as getting married, buying insurance, and getting a job.

You may already have a CURP number! Even if you don't think you have one, your parents may have registered you when you were a baby. You can search for it online here: www.consultas.curp.gob.mx.

You will be asked for your name, sex, and place of birth. If you find yourself in the system, perfect! Check that your information is correct and download the certificate from the website. It's a good idea to print a couple of copies for your files.

If the website says you don't have one, it will offer to let you print a certificate of non-existence ("Constancia de inexistencia"). Print it out and bring it with you to request your CURP. This will make the process easier.

How to Request Your CURP

If you find that you do not have a CURP, go in person to a CURP office. See this site for locations: www.gob.mx/cms/uploads/attachment/file/39942/DirectoriodeModulosCURP.pdf. They do not take appointments. It is a good idea to go early in the morning. Check their opening and closing hours before you go.

Bring the following with you:

- Your birth certificate
- Your official photo ID (INE)
- Your certificate of non-existence ("Constancia de inexistencia") that shows you do not have a CURP

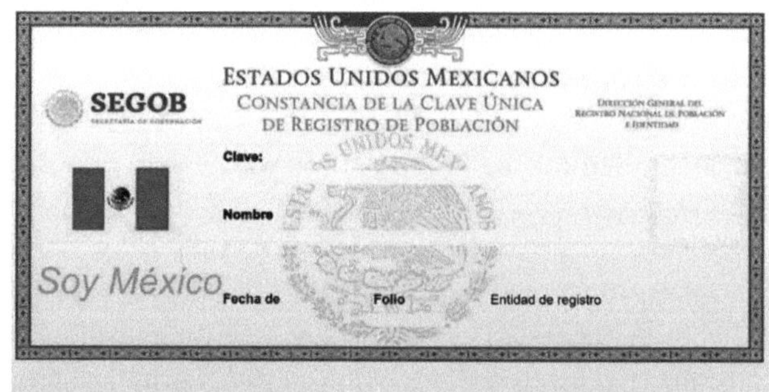

After receiving your CURP, it's a good idea to make a copy.

RFC (Registro Federal de Contribuyentes)

The RFC stands for Federal Taxpayers Registry. It is a number that the government assigns to you to pay taxes. The tax service in Mexico is called the SAT or "Tributary Administration Service."

The RFC is required for everyone 18 years and over. You must have one even if you don't have a job that requires you to pay taxes. It's one of your most important documents. You'll need it to open bank accounts, get a job, buy property, use social programs and scholarships, and more.

You can request your RFC online here: https://www54.sat.gob.mx/curp/Consult. You can also get your RFC at any SAT (tax) office or by calling (800) 463-6728.

Military Card

If you're male between the ages of 18 and 40, you must register for the military. Women can register if they want to. When you register, you'll get a military card which is free and has many benefits.

You can visit your local town hall (ayuntamiento or alcaldía) to see what the dates are for registering for military service.

To register you'll go to the military recruitment office and give them:

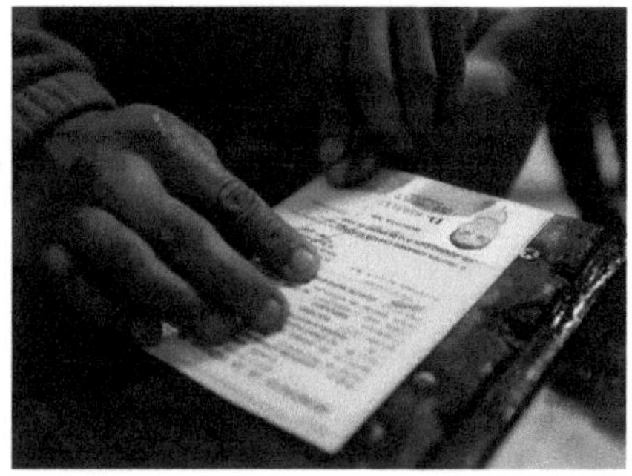

- Four recent 35 x 45 mm photos. You can get these done at any photo studio and at some pharmacies by asking for a "foto infantil." They will ask you not to wear a hat or jewelry. They know all the other specifics required for this ID photo.
- Birth certificate, original and copy
- Proof of address, original and copy
- Proof of highest level of school
- CURP, original and copy
- Universal National Military Service Form, available here: http://www.sedena.gob.mx/archivos/formatos_comprometidos/Formato_Universal_SMN.pdf

Learn more: https://www.gob.mx/sedena/acciones-y-programas/cuales-son-los-requisitos-para-tramitar-la-cartilla-de-identidad-del-servicio-militar

Driver's License

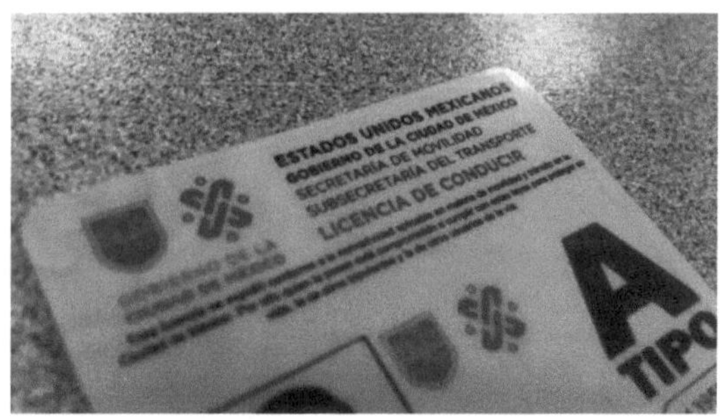

If you plan on driving in Mexico, you will need a driver's license. There are three kinds of licenses:

- Regular or "automovilística"
- Driver up to three tons
- Commercial

Each state has its own driver's licenses. The name of the agency where you get your license is different in every state. In some states it's called the Secretary of Infrastructure, Mobility and Transport. In other states the name is Secretary of Mobility, and in others it's the Secretary of Communication and Transport. The age and requirements for a license are different in every state.

Many states let you make an appointment by calling or using their website. Check with your local agency to see what you need to bring. You will probably need your:

- Birth certificate
- Current official ID, like your INE, passport, or military card
- Proof of address
- CURP
- Receipt for payment of fees. Check with your state to find out the fee and how to pay it. Some states let you pay online and print off your proof of payment. Others have a form that you can take to a bank or local pharmacy or quick stop store and pay.
- Proof of blood type
- Written test. Here's a preview of what you can expect to find on the test: https://www.univision.com/noticias/autos/aprobarias-de-nuevo-el-examen-de-manejo
- Some states require a driving test and a medical exam.

☆ For details on getting a license in Mexico City visit: https://www.semovi.cdmx.gob.mx/tramites-y-servicios/vehiculos-particulares/automovil/licencias

Passport

You'll need a passport if you plan to go out of the country. Make an appointment ahead of time by calling (800) 801-0773 or online: citas.sre.gob.mx

Bring the following with you:

- Certified copy of your birth certificate (original),
- INE or other current photo ID (original and copy),
- A passport photo
- Proof of payment. You can pay at any local bank after you print the payment form from this website: https://www.gob.mx/pasaporte

☆ You can get a passport that is good for one year, three years, six years, or 10 years. Costs range from 755 pesos to 1,755 pesos. You will save money if you choose a longer time frame. If you are over 60 years old, disabled, or a temporary farm worker, you are eligible for a 50% discount on the costs.

Whenever completing any "tramite" (bureaucratic process or procedure), bring all original documents as well as two copies. This will keep you from losing your place in line by having to leave to make copies. An even better idea is to bring a file with all your important documents to official government offices, "por si las dudas" (just in case)!

Héroes Paisanos Program

https://www.gob.mx/heroespaisanos

The Héroes Paisanos program helps returning citizens with:

- Collecting identity documents
- Registering for medical insurance, food assistance, and shelter
- Offering free phone calls to family members
- Transportation
- Providing information about job opportunities, including grants to start businesses
- Educational support
- Individual case manager support

You can sign up for the program through The National Immigration Institute (INM) office in your state. For a list of offices visit: https://www.inm.gob.mx/gobmx/word/index.php/horarios-y-oficinas/

This program also publishes a guide (in Spanish) to help returning citizens. You can see the full guide here: www.gob.mx/cms/uploads/attachment/file/45147/GUIA_SOMOS_MEXICANOS_PRIM.pdf

The Paisano Guide is also very useful and can be accessed here (in Spanish): https://www.gob.mx/cms/uploads/attachment/file/595749/GUIA_PAISANO_2020.pdf

It can also be downloaded to your device through the code above.

Resources to Meet Basic Needs

You probably have plans and dreams for your future. Still, day-to-day life might be hard. Many deported people struggle with finding housing, getting a job, and paying for things. Others have trouble with drug and alcohol addictions and mental health issues. Be patient as you figure things out. There are programs and people who can help.

Cost of Living Expenses

Things are much cheaper in Mexico than the US. You can see a doctor for free in Mexico's universal health care program or for 45 pesos ($2.20 USD) otherwise!

Electricity is run by the government, which makes it cheaper. The more electricity you use, the more it will cost you. Save money by using low-energy light bulbs, turning off lights, and unplugging appliances.

Cell phones are much cheaper than in the US. Landlines for local calls are even cheaper.

While most things are cheaper in Mexico, gasoline is not. It's often more than in the US and goes up every year. Clothing also tends to cost more and is lower quality. Clothing at many common chain stores (Suburbia, for example) won't last long. It might be a good idea to buy fewer clothes that are better quality. They will last longer.

Need Assistance?
Here are a few places to start:

Food. Most major cities in Mexico have at least one soup kitchen or "comedor." See the directory in the back of this guide for locations.

Health care. The government provides a health care program for Mexican citizens called **INSABI** (Institute of Health for Wellbeing), formerly "Seguro Popular." Learn how to apply by consulting the Health chapter. Visit a hospital, non-profit organization, church, or state agency and ask for help. See our Directory.

Addictions. Groups such as Narcotics Anonymous and Alcoholics Anonymous can assist you with addiction recovery. For a list of offices, go to www.aamexico.org.mx or www.narcoticosanonimos.org.mx

Food

Government soup kitchens. The government offers hot meals at soup kitchens called "comedores" every day. In Mexico City, there are two types:

- "Comedores comunitarios," or "community soup kitchens" charge 11 pesos (about 65 cents) for meals. They are open to anyone living in high-poverty areas, people over 65, children, pregnant women, people with disabilities, people without jobs, and people who are homeless.
- "Comedores públicos," or "public soup kitchens" serve the same groups of people, but are free. You will need to enroll to get meals.

For more information on soup kitchens in Mexico City see: https://www.sds.cdmx.gob.mx/programa-comedores-sociales

Church soup kitchens. Many churches have soup kitchens as well. For example, the Cathedral of Mexico City offers meals on Saturday mornings. Check with your local Catholic archdiocese to see if they can help (https://www.catholicdirectory.com/mexico/diocese). You can also do an internet search for "comedores" in your area.

Social Milk Program. This government program will give you and your family up to four liters a week of quality milk at low cost. To sign up, you will need an official ID, proof of address, birth certificates, and CURP numbers for you and your family. Locate the Liconsa point of sale or dairy closest to your home and find out when they are open. Learn more: https://www.gob.mx/tramites/ficha/incorporacion-al-padron-de-beneficiarios-del-programa-de-abasto-social-de-leche/LICONSA1471

Healthcare

INSABI (Institute of Health for Wellbeing)

INSABI is a Mexico healthcare program for all citizens who do not have access to other health care. It is most often used by Mexicans who are not employed or who cannot afford other health insurance. INSABI covers 57 million Mexicans.

The program provides medical, surgery, pharmacy, and hospital services. It will cover expensive illnesses and life-threatening emergencies.

To get help, go to a public hospital or clinic. Bring your personal documents: your CURP, INE and birth certificate.

For the location nearest you see the directory. For more information on INSABI, see the Health chapter.

Mental Health and Substance Use

(See the Health chapter for more information.)

If you struggle with mental health or substance use, try to get support. Sadly, INSABI does not cover mental health and substance use, but there are other places to get help.

- **Therapy.** Your local DIF (Desarrollo Integral de la Familia) office may offer low-cost therapy. Here's a directory of DIF locations in Mexico City: https://dif.cdmx.gob.mx/directorio-de-centros-dif-cdmx. Do an online search for "DIF" and the name of your town or city. There are also other places to get therapy, some low-cost. Most pharmacies have a list of service providers.
- **Support groups.** If you have drug or alcohol problems, join a support group such as Alcoholics Anonymous (www.aamexico.org.mx) or Narcotics Anonymous (www.narcoticosanonimos.org.mx). It will be hard to take care of the other areas of your life if you have drug or alcohol challenges.

Government Support Programs

The Mexican government offers support programs for people who need help. These programs can change often, so check to see if they are still open.

- **Single Mother Support Program.** This program provides a monthly payment to working mothers with children ages 1-4. See https://www.gob.mx/bienestar/acciones-y-programas/programa-de-apoyo-para-el-bienestar-de-las-ninas-y-ninos-hijos-de-madres-trabajadoras-203284
- **Program for Individuals with Disabilities.** This program offers a monthly payment to people who can't work because of a disability. https://www.gob.mx/bienestar/acciones-y-programas/programa-pension-para-el-bienestar-de-las-personas-con-discapacidad
- **Senior Support Program** provides a monthly payment to people above retirement age. https://www.gob.mx/bienestar/acciones-y-programas/programa-para-el-bienestar-de-las-personas-adultas-mayores
- **Benito Juarez Wellbeing Grants** This program pays families of school-age children 800 a month during the school year. https://www.gob.mx/becasbenitojuarez

Housing

If you have family in Mexico you may want to stay with them at first. Mexico is very family-oriented. It's common for many relatives to live in one house. You may even want to live with distant relatives. Consider your options carefully. Where will you have family or friends to help you? Do you like a big city or a small town? Which areas have the kinds of jobs you are looking for?

Safety

Much of Mexico is less developed than the US. It's very important to feel safe where you decide to live. Is it well lit? Does your building offer security? No matter where you live, there are a few things you can do to stay safe.

- Always be aware of what's going on around you.
- Don't show off your money or wear flashy jewelry.
- Don't use electronics while walking down the street.
- Change the lock on the place you rent as soon as you move in.

Renting a Place

Costs. The cost of housing depends on where you live. If you don't have a lot of money, you can rent a room in a shared house. Look for signs posted on telephone poles or at small businesses. Renting a room can cost between $50 and $100 USD a month (1,000-2,000 pesos). If you rent your own apartment, you can expect to pay up to 5,000 or 7,000 pesos.

Finding an apartment. Most people find rooms or apartments by word of mouth or by responding to ads. Here are a few websites that may help:

- https://www.trovit.com.mx/
- www.vivanuncios.com.mx
- https://www.inmuebles24.com/

Once you've found a place you like, call the landlord and set up a time to see it. Arrive on time and dress nice. Cover any tattoos if you can. It may take some time before you find a room or apartment you like. Don't be discouraged! Once you find one, let the owner or property manager know of your interest.

Rental contract. Make sure to ask for a rental contract to protect yourself. Simple rental contract forms are available at neighborhood stationary stores.

Security deposits. A security deposit is money that you pay to a landlord before moving into a room or apartment. The landlord keeps this money, even if you decide not to move into it. There is no limit to how much a landlord can charge for a security deposit. Usually, landlords charge one month's rent. It is important to get a lease in writing before paying a landlord and to also get a receipt after paying.

Just like in the US, security deposits are used by landlords to cover damage to the apartment after you leave. The security deposit is not used for regular wear and tear, but for big things, like a cracked window or broken light. When you move in, take photos of any damage you notice. Let the owner or manager know about these things so that you don't have to pay for them later. You should get a receipt for specific damages at the end of your stay. Your landlord will give you the rest of your security deposit the day you move out. Sometimes the landlord will use the security deposit to pay for the last month's rent. Before paying the last month's rent, ask your landlord if they expect you to pay it or not.

☆ A note about public housing in Mexico:
The Mexican government offers much less housing support than it used to. There are a few organizations that help families build low-cost housing, including Habitat for Humanity (www.habitatmexico.org) and Échale México (www.echale.com.mx).

Breaking a lease. If you need to move out before your lease has expired, you can do so. However, you will have to pay a fee for breaking the lease. The amount that you will pay will normally be listed in the lease.

Some examples of questions you could ask the landlord during your visit:

- What is the monthly rent?
- Are utilities included?
- When is the rent due?
- What is the parking situation?
- Are tenants able to make small changes? (e.g., paint the walls)

Take your time. Get a plan together to achieve short and long-term goals. Ask questions. Everything changes, so ask and learn.

—Brian N.

The advice I would give is to be patient. Things in the outside world move very quickly and I think that you have to be aware and accept that you don't have to catch up.

—Oscar S.

Transportation

How are you going to get around? You may need transportation to get to a job, visit family and friends, and more. If you return to Mexico City, you'll have many options. The city has a good metro system that charges just 5 pesos per ride (about 25 cents). It also has metro buses, regular buses, taxis, bikes and Uber.

Here are a few options for getting around.

Buses and Metro

You can save money by using public transportation. Ask people whether it's safe to use public transportation in your area. Try not to travel late at night by yourself. In some cities, buses have been the target of robberies.

In Mexico City as well as in other major cities, there are "metro buses." These buses use special lanes, making them faster. In Mexico City, riders buy a card and recharge it. Rides are 5 pesos.

Mexico City's subway is the cheapest in the world at just 25 cents, or 5 pesos. It is efficient but crowded. Stay aware and carry your valuables in a safe place. Do not keep them in your back pocket. For a map of Mexico City's subway system please see the next page or download the "Metrobus Mexico" app for your smartphone. The app also covers Monterrey and Guadalajara.

Carpool and Rideshare Programs

You can save money with carpool and rideshare programs. Talk to family, friends, coworkers, and neighbors about driving together and sharing the cost of gas. You can also look up carpool programs online. See https://www.carpoolworld.com/carpool_list_cities.html?country_code=MEX,MX&state_code=&start_at=0&page_no=1

Taxis and Ride-Hailing Apps.

You can take taxis in cities and towns across Mexico, but they are not always safe. Always take a taxi from an authorized taxi stand or booth. Do not hail taxis or go with someone trying to get your business. Outside of train stations and metro stops you will hear people calling "taxi? taxi?" Their rides are expensive and could be scams.

Ride-hailing apps are fairly new. If you have a smartphone and a credit or debit card, you can download ride-hailing apps like Uber to take short trips in your city. They may not be available everywhere, though. Ride-hailing apps are just like taxis, but the drivers work for themselves. Just like taxis, they can be unsafe. Before you ride, read these tips on how to use the app safely. www.uber.com/us/en/ride/safety/tips/

Biking

Biking is a good way to save money, explore, and get fit. But it can be very dangerous in big cities. If you choose to bike, always wear a helmet, and be alert. Make sure your bike has reflectors and lights if you ride at night, and wear light, easy-to-see clothing.

It may seem that most drivers and cyclists are not following the rules. Remember, you put yourself and others in serious danger if you don't. Bicycles should follow most of the same rules as cars. They must stop at stop signs and traffic lights. Use hand signals to switch lanes or make a turn. And yield to pedestrians.

In Mexico City, you can rent bikes (see www.ecobici.cdmx.gob.mx). If you want to buy your own bike, look for second-hand bike stores. This site helps you plan your bike route in Mexico City: www.bbbike.org/MexicoCity

Cars

If you need to buy a car to get around, be careful. Car payments in Mexico go from 3,500 to more than 7,000 pesos per month, even for a used car.

☆ A note about buying from individuals:

Many people in Mexico buy cars from other people. Make sure they are people you know and trust. Take the car to a mechanic so you know what issues the car might have. Be sure to get copies of the seller's ID and proof of address. Make sure you have a letter of sale filled out according to the laws of your state. You can find these letters in neighborhood stationary shops. If you do not know the person you are buying from, check with local police to make sure the car is not stolen.

Keeping your car legal in Mexico

In Mexico you need current plates. Many states also require an annual sticker with its own tax as well as an additional annual fee. In most states you must pay a fee for a smog check. If you plan on driving in Mexico City, be aware of what days you are allowed to drive your car. Due to extreme air pollution, certain license plate numbers cannot drive on certain days. There are many limits on out-of-state vehicles in Mexico City as well. When smog is very bad, this restriction will include even more days. See www.hoy-no-circula.com.mx

Mexico City Metro (Sistema de Transporte Collectivo)
System Diagram

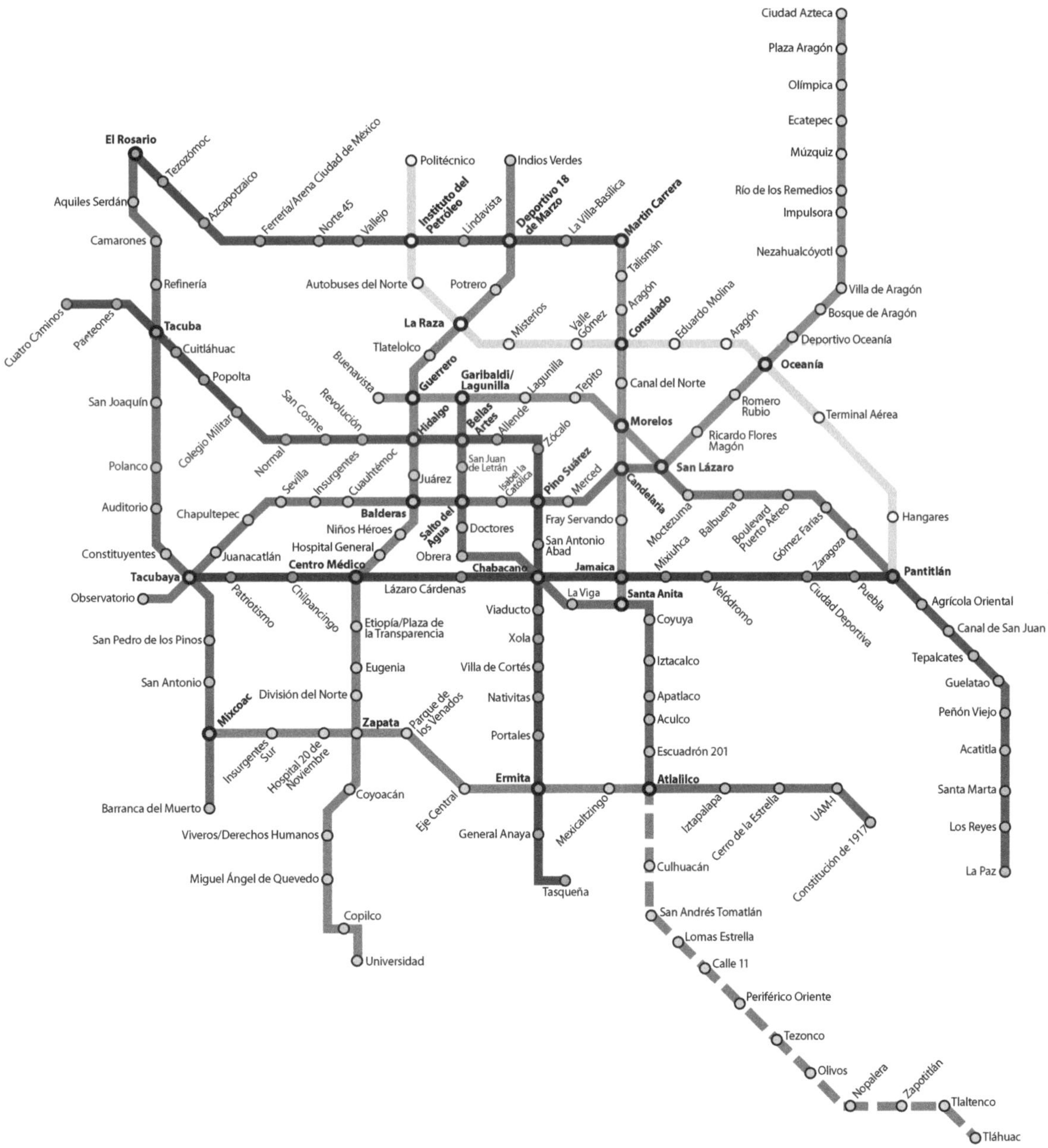

Employment

Are you worried about finding a job after deportation? Maybe you're worried you won't make a lot of money in your new country. The good news is that being deported to Mexico probably won't hurt your reputation. You can get good jobs because of the skills you gained during your time in the US.

The cost of living in Mexico and Central America is low. You won't need to make as much as you did in the US. Stay persistent in your job search. Open yourself to different kinds of opportunities. If you do this, you will find work. It may just take longer than you expected.

This chapter includes the following sections:

- Thinking about your job search
- Recommended job opportunities
- Employment help and training opportunities
- Finding a job
- Stipends and programs that offer cash assistance in Mexico
- Building a long-term career

Expect to have mixed feelings about your situation. Right now I have everything but at the same time I don't have anything (car, TV, house).

—Alex A.

Thinking About Your Job Search

You probably have a lot on your plate. You're looking for a job, finding a place to stay, reconnecting with loved ones, and getting used to a new country. It is hard to do all of this at once! Think of your first few jobs after your return as "transition jobs." These transition jobs will help you make money. They can also help you move you into a career that you enjoy. They might not pay much, and they might not be jobs you love. But they will help you get where you want to go.

Building the career you want takes many years and many different jobs. Don't be discouraged. Keep your eye on the big picture. For long-term career advice see the Employment chapter.

If you have a criminal record. If you have a record in the US, it will likely not follow you. In parts of Mexico away from the border, background checks are uncommon.

If you work for a US company in Mexico or you work in a border town, the company may run a background check. Keep this in mind as you think about which jobs may be a good fit for you. If you do have a record, be honest about what types of jobs fit you best. There could be jobs where you might be at risk of doing things that get you in trouble. Unlike in the US, you will not have a parole officer making sure you are on the right track. This will be your responsibility, and it's important to take it seriously.

Recommended Job Opportunities

The money people make in Mexico is less than in the US. The daily minimum wage is 173 pesos or about $8 USD. The good news is there are many ways to earn more money. Below, we list a few job options, recommended by people who have been recently deported.

Self employment or starting your own business. In Mexico, opening a business is easier and cheaper than in the US. Many people sell things in the street, open small shops, or do things like cleaning and auto detailing. You can open a shop in the front room of your house. You can also rent a commercial space. Renting a commercial space is very cheap, and the first year of your new business is tax-free.

As in the US, there are risks to starting your own business. You will notice that a salon, restaurant, or car wash is here one month and gone the next. It's important to have a business plan. You also need to make sure you have enough money to start a business. The US Chamber of Commerce offers guidance on how to write a business plan on their website: https://www.uschamber.com/co/start/startup/writing-business-plan-guide.

Inform yourself before you invest any money in a business. Think about the type of business you want to start and be sure there is really a need. Consider location. If you want to start a laundry or a restaurant, choose an area where there will not be much competition.

—Oscar S.

Work in a manufacturing job. In the north of Mexico there are many jobs in factories, called "maquiladoras." All types of goods are made in Mexico and sold in the US. Many things are made in Mexico because the workers are paid much less. The current rate at the border is 312 pesos or $17 US a day. In the rest of the country the rate is 207 pesos, or $11.50 US. Further south, companies like Volkswagen and Audi have opened factories. They may pay more money, depending on the job. There are opportunities to work for Mexican-owned companies, too, of course.

☆ **A note about working in call centers and factories at the border:** Many recently deported people choose to work in low-paid jobs at factories or at call centers. They pay a little more than minimum wage. Beware of the possibility of getting stuck. It may be best to treat them as transition jobs and keep searching for better jobs.

If at first you can't find a job, keep looking, keep asking, keep knocking. In Mexico there's work; you just have to have a positive attitude, and don't give up.

—Ramon C.

10 Largest Employers in Mexico	
Walmart	Supermarket chain
FEMSA	The largest beverage business in Mexico and Latin America
Grupo Bimbo	Mexican baking company
PepsiCo	American food, snack, and beverage corporation
BBVA	Banking and financial services
CitiBanamex	Banking and financial services
Grupo Financiero Banorte	Second biggest finance and banking group in Mexico
Banco Santander	Banking and financial services
Stellantis	Manufacturing corporation
Nissan Motor Corporation	Global car manufacturer

For Bilingual Speakers

If you speak both English and Spanish, you may be able to get a job that pays more.

English teaching. There is a big need for people to teach English in public or private schools. If you know English grammar or have worked as a teaching assistant or tutor, this will help you get a job. Even without this experience, you can get a job in places with few English speakers. Often, an intermediate English level and some classes are enough to teach in Mexico.

Some schools might ask you to take an English proficiency test from your local university. You will receive a certificate, known as a "constancia," that will allow you to work in local schools.

If you want to work with adults, many private schools offer English classes in the evenings. When you tell people you speak English, they may ask you to give them classes or teach their children. You could promote yourself as a teacher and offer private tutoring.

Major English schools in Mexico include:

- Interlingua
- Harmon Hall
- Berlitz
- Quicklearning

For a list of English schools in Mexico City visit https://www.anders.com.mx/main-escuelas-ingles-cdmx.html

If your English is strong, you may be able to teach English online, especially if you have teaching experience. Many people all over the world want to learn English.

If you feel good about promoting yourself, consider teaching freelance online. Sites like www.italki.com allow you to set your own hours, rate ($4-80 USD/hour) and use your own materials. You can call yourself either a "professional English teacher" or a "community tutor." A community tutor helps people practice through conversations. Italki takes 15% of what you make.

You may also have luck working for an English school online. For more information and resources for teaching English online visit goodairlanguage.com.

You don't have to be an expert in English grammar or ESL to make this a good career. Charisma and ability to keep students engaged are more important than English grammar. Most of the time people want to learn vocabulary and pronunciation. Being a native English speaker is usually an advantage. Here is a list of companies that hire advanced non-native speakers: www.goodairlanguage.com/non-native.

Work for a call center. Bilingual call centers offer customer service, technical support, and even debt collection for many companies in the United States. This is a large industry in Mexico. Many of the people who work in them are Mexicans who have lived in the United States and speak English well. You usually need an intermediate level of English. Call centers are in major cities in Mexico, including Puebla, Mexico City, Tijuana, and Nuevo Laredo.

Work for the tourist industry. If you speak English and Spanish you can find work in hotels and resorts. They need restaurant servers, cab and tour bus drivers, and tour guides. You could also work as a club promoter, housekeeper, or at a museum or tourist attraction.

Major tourist areas in Mexico include:

- The Cancun/Cozumel/Riviera Maya area, Quintana Roo
- Tijuana, Rosarito, and Ensenada, Baja California Norte
- Los Cabos, Baja California Sur
- Mazatlán, Sinaloa
- Huatulco and Puerto Escondido, Oaxaca
- Acapulco, Guerrero
- Puerto Vallarta, Jalisco and Riviera Nayarit areas

Work in the airport. Airports and airlines need bilingual employees to help travelers and sell tickets.

Work online. Working online can be a good way to make a lot of money, especially if you can find a job that pays in dollars. With the exchange rate at about 17 pesos to the dollar, you can see why! There are several international online companies that hire bilingual people. They need people to evaluate ads, online searches, and social media posts. These companies include appen.com and www.lionbridge.com. For more information, see https://thisonlineworld.com/sites-like-appen/. At home sales may be another option for you.

Other professionals. Businesses are also looking for people who speak English and Spanish to work in human resources, as administrative assistants, and in logistics. Some of these positions require a degree.

Computer/software Engineering Jobs

There are many jobs in computers that let you work from home. These jobs are in software engineering, coding, or computer programming. You might see all of these words used to mean the same thing. You may not need a lot of education to get a job in computer programming. It's pretty easy and cheap to get the training you need for an entry-level computer programming job.

There are lots of YouTube videos and resources on the internet for free that can help you learn a computer language. They go all the way from beginner's level to a professional level (e.g. codecademy.com, w3schools.com, codewars.com). Your progression will depend on the time you invest and your ability to process and analyze information in a logical manner. All computer programs are based on logic. How well you do will depend on how well you can use computer logic. The more time you put in, the sooner you will finish your training.

There are two languages that you need to learn:

- HTML (Hypertext Markup Language https:// www.youtube.com/watch?v=UB1O3OfR-EE). HTML handles what is displayed on your browser.
- CSS (Cascading Style Sheets https://www.youtube.com/watch?v=yfoY53QXEnI). CSS is what allows you to style your page display.

Other languages you could learn to help you get a job include:

- Java: https://www.youtube.com/watch?v=Qgl81fPcLc8
- JavaScript: https://www.youtube.com/watch?v=jS4aFq5-91M
- Python: https://www.youtube.com/watch?v=WGJJIrtnfpk
- C#: https://www.youtube.com/watch?v=FPeGkedZykA
- C++: https://www.youtube.com/watch?v=GQp1zzTwrIg
- PHP: https://www.youtube.com/watch?v=2eebptXfEvw

There are lots of free resources on the internet. But you can also pay for classes with places like Udemy (udemy.com) and Coursera (es.coursera.org). They offer full courses on specific languages. Many of these courses are cheap–usually no more than $15 US. They are very good classes.

Employment Help and Training Opportunities

People in Mexico want to help people who return. There are lots of government programs for returning citizens to find work, get training, and rebuild their lives. Here are a few programs that help people with jobs.

- **The National Employment Service** (Servicio Nacional de Empleo, or SNE) helps connect workers and employers around the country. Their services include job postings, occupational orientation, financial support and training, and emergency response services. They organize job fairs and workshops on how to find a job. They also offer counseling for job placement. For more information: https://www.gob.mx/empleo. To schedule an interview, call (333) 668-1681, M-F, 10am-5pm, or email them at: snebolsadetrabajo@gmail.com.
- **Mexico Secretary of Labor** This national department of labor has a lot of job programs. "Youth Building the Future" (Jóvenes construyendo el futuro) places young people in paid internships. They work the internship for a year and learn job skills. https://jovenesconstruyendoelfuturo.stps.gob.mx/ You can find information on more programs here: https://www.gob.mx/stps
- **Mexico City Secretary of Labor** Mexico City has its own employment department. They run job fairs, post opportunities, and provide information about your rights as a worker. https://www.trabajo.cdmx.gob.mx/
- **Héroes Paisanos Program** This program mostly helps returning citizens with immediate needs. But they also offer information on job opportunities. They give people grants to start businesses, and can help you with individual case manager support. For more information visit https://www.gob.mx/heroespaisanos.
- **Social Economy Support Program** (Programa de fomento a la economía social). This program provides money for people with low-income to run projects. What they give you will depend on your needs and ideas. The program is open to people in small towns (15,000 people or less) where there are not many job options. They award grants of up to 25,000 pesos for each person employed. The most you can get for your grant is between 300,000 and 5 million pesos. For more information, download an application at: www.gob.mx/cms/uploads/attachment/file/30101/Anexo_2.pdf
  Requirements: www.gob.mx/cms/uploads/attachment/file/44576/ROP2016.pdf
- **The Carlos Slim Foundation** offers free online education and job training certificates through their app aprende.org. You can get diplomas and certificates in accounting, construction, food service, renewable energy, health and technology, among others.
- **TEFL Programs.** There are many Teaching English as a Foreign Language (TEFL) programs in Mexico that offer certificates: https://www.eslbase.com/tefl-courses/mexico/. You can also get a TEFL certificate for about $40 USD at www.groupon.com/deals/n-learn-tefl-120-hour-tefl-course. The most respected certificate is from Cambridge University and costs about $1,000 USD. For more information visit www.cambridgeenglish.org/find-a-centre/find-an-exam-centre/
- **Growing Life Program** (Programa Sembrando Vida). This program helps people in the country who own at least 2.5 hectares of land. If you want to cultivate or reforest the land, they will help you. For more information, including requirements, visit https://www.gob.mx/bienestar/acciones-y-programas/programa-sembrando-vida

Finding a Job

Networking

There are many ways to find jobs. Networking is probably the most important. Networking means talking to many, many different people who can help you find jobs. The people you talk to may not have a job for you right now. But they could give you career advice. They might know someone who knows someone else with a job lead. They might learn of a job in the future. Tell your friends, family, and others you know about what kind of job you want. Talk to friends and neighbors about your job search.

One good strategy is to talk to people who have the kind of job you want to do. Ask them for ideas, suggestions, and information that can help you find job leads. The power of face-to-face interaction is huge, especially if you're friendly.

Online Searches

You can also search for jobs online. Websites that publish jobs in Mexico include:

- Occmundial (occ.com.mx)
- Trovit (empleo.trovit.com.mx)
- Computrabajo (computrabajo.com.mx)
- Indeed (mx.indeed.com)
- Bumeran (bumeran.com.mx)

These websites are important if you want to work for a large employer. But these sites are much less important than they used to be. Visit the websites of places you want to work and find the jobs posted there. Often, you will find a link to "Current Jobs" ("oferta de empleo" o "bolsa de trabajo") on the home page.

Companies in Mexico don't always list open jobs. Contact the company directly to ask if there is a job opening.

LinkedIn is a very good place to connect to professional jobs. It is a professional social network, a place where you can connect with people who work where you would like to work. Head to www.linkedin.com to make a profile and review job postings (see the "jobs" link below the search bar at the top of every page).

When searching for a job online, be careful of scams. Scammers may ask for money or your personal information like your birthday, ID number or debit/credit card number. Never give out your personal information on the internet.

Job fairs

City governments hold job fairs. In Mexico City the branch that deals with employment is called, in Spanish, "La Secretaría del Trabajo y Fomento al Empleo de la CDMX" (or STyFE). Information about job fairs can be found at: www.trabajo.cdmx.gob.mx

If you don't live in Mexico City, be sure and check your city's webpage for job fair and job training information. See our directory for these and more resources in your community.

Keep Records

It is a good idea to keep a record of all the places you have applied to. Record any visits you made in person, first phone calls, and follow-up phone calls. Here is an example log you can use:

Example Job Application Log	
Name of position	
Company name and contact info	
Application date	
Response date	
Interview date	
Name(s) and contact info of interviewers	
Thank you letter date	
Notes	

The Application Process

Job Application Forms

The purpose of a job application is to get you a job interview. Employers use job applications to decide who is worth talking to in-person. The best way to get an interview is to focus on the positives. What do you have to offer an employer? Don't focus on negatives like poor work history or limited education. Most employers do not have a lot of time to read every application. In fact, most hiring managers will look at your application for about 15 to 30 seconds. They are looking for a form that is neat and complete. Many businesses will want you to submit a complete, generic job application form that can be found in "papelerías" or small stationary stores throughout Mexico. See the Solicitud de Empleo in the Additional Resources section for an example.

The "Employment" or "Previous Employment" section is usually the most detailed section of a job application.

Here are some tips on filling out an application:
Do you see the "work performed" or "job duties" section? Use the whole space to list your skills, accomplishments, and contributions you made in your past jobs. Do not list your wages from past jobs. Wages in the US will not be similar to the wages in your home country. Give a positive reason for leaving all previous jobs, even if you quit or were let go. Think about what happened after, did you get a new job? Did you start a training program or go to school?

The job application will also usually ask for the following:

References. References are people who can say that you're responsible and a good worker. Employers usually ask for three references. Who should you list as a reference? Do not list family members. Good references can come from previous and current employers, bosses, teachers, social workers, people you have volunteered with, and people from your religious institution. It's ok to list references from the US. It's best to pick ones who speak at least some Spanish.

Criminal History. Does the application ask if you have a criminal record? If you do, you may want to check "yes." Then write, "will discuss at the interview." Talking about your history on the application might hurt your application. Wait until the interview so you can share how you have taken responsibility for your actions, what you have learned from the situation, and how you are different today. And remember, discrimination based on criminal record is illegal in Mexico.

Resumes and Cover Letters

Your resume maps out your job history. It gives details about your past jobs, your skills, and your interests. You will submit the same resume to each employer. In Spanish the document is known as "currículum."

Many employers will want a resume and cover letter with your application. Your cover letter is an actual letter from you to each employer. It tells a short story about who you are, why you are looking for a job, your background, and what's important to you. Keep your letter to one page.

Writing good resumes and cover letters takes time. Start working on them long before you apply for your first job.

☆ Two great websites for resume and cover letter preparation are:

- https://owl.purdue.edu/owl/about_the_owl/owl_information/index.html
- https://extension.harvard.edu/blog/how-to-write-a-great-resume-and-cover-letter/

Examples of a resume and cover letter from someone who has been incarcerated and deported can be found in the Additional Resources section.

Interviews

Once you've sent an application to an employer, wait to be contacted. Hopefully, they will be interested in interviewing with you. But remember, most applications do not lead to interviews. Be patient. Keep sending out applications until you have an actual job offer. Many job seekers are nervous about interviews. They want to say the right things and make a good impression. Practice what you'll say, and consider the following tips:

Bring the right materials. Bring copies of your resume, contact information for your references, and any papers you need to finish your application. These might be copies of work licenses, your driving record (if required), and INE and CURP. Bring a pen and notebook to write down information. It shows that you are truly interested in the job.

Arrive 10 to 15 minutes early for your interview. You might need to fill out paperwork before the interview. Finding the right person or room could take longer than you think. Arriving early shows you are responsible and eager to be there.

Wear appropriate clothes. Wear something a bit more formal than what you would wear for the job. Think about your body language. Even when you are not speaking, you are sending a message. Make good eye contact, stand and sit tall, smile, and shake hands firmly.

Ask questions. At the end of a job interview, most hiring managers will ask something like "Do you have any questions for me?" Strong job candidates always have a few questions ready. Asking questions makes you seem interested in the job, rather than desperate. If you brought a pen and notebook with you, you could make a list of questions in the back of the notebook.

Some examples of questions you could ask:

- What is the organization's plan for the next five years?
- How will I be evaluated, and in what time frames? By whom?
- What are the day-to-day responsibilities of this job?
- What computer equipment and software do you use?
- When will a decision be made about this position?

Some examples of positive reasons for leaving:

- You moved.
- You wanted a career change.
- You became a full-time student.
- The work was seasonal.
- You had the opportunity to advance.

Employment discrimination is a serious problem in Mexico. It is illegal for businesses to hire people based on things like age and gender. But many still do. You'll even see help wanted signs only for people of a particular gender or age. You may be worried about not getting a job because of your age. But keep in mind that Mexico is a country of small business owners, much more so than the US. You'll see people offering services out of the front rooms of their houses, from dentists to mechanics.

Think of this as an opportunity. What skills do you have? What skills can you develop? What space will you have in Mexico where you could start a small business? Do you know anyone self-employed? They may be able to help you get started. Once you get that business started, you may even be able to offer a job to someone else! That said, there is a government agency where you can report employment discrimination if you do face it. In Spanish it's called "Secretaría del Trabajo y Previsión Social." www.gob.mx/stps/prensa/atiende-stps-quejas-laborales-a-traves-del-centro-de-mando

Programs that Offer Cash Assistance in Mexico

In Mexico, there are programs that provide money to people who need support. They include the following:

- **Single Mother Support Program.** This program provides a monthly payment to working mothers with children between one and four years old. For more information visit: https://www.gob.mx/bienestar/acciones-y-programas/programa-de-apoyo-para-el-bienestar-de-las-ninas-y-ninos-hijos-de-madres-trabajadoras-203284
- **Program for Individuals with Disabilities.** This program offers a monthly payment to people who can't work because of a disability. https://www.gob.mx/bienestar/acciones-y-programas/programa-pension-para-el-bienestar-de-las-personas-con-discapacidad
- **Senior Support Program.** This program provides a monthly payment to people over retirement age. https://www.gob.mx/bienestar/acciones-y-programas/programa-para-el-bienestar-de-las-personas-adultas-mayores

In the US, unemployment insurance is available to everyone. This is not the case in Mexico. But there are a few programs. Some are run by the federal government and others by the state. Several states have begun unemployment programs in response to COVID-19. To find out if your state has one, search for the name of the state and key terms like "seguro de desempleo" (unemployment insurance) or "apoyo de desempleo" (unemployment support).

Mexico City Unemployment Benefit (Programa seguro de desempleo de la Ciudad de México)

Unemployment benefits are available to people in Mexico City for up to six months. The benefit includes a monthly payment at the minimum wage for full time work–2,925 pesos, roughly $170 USD.

To qualify for the benefit, you must be over 18 and live in Mexico City. You must not have a job, but you must be looking for one. You must not receive other income transfers, such as a pension. The program's goal is to help workers get jobs and training.

Requirements:

- Must apply in person.
- Benefit is non-transferable.
- Must have returned to live in Mexico City after January 1, 2017.
- Must be between 18 and 68 years of age.
- Must receive no other income such as retirement benefits, pension, subsidy neither in Mexico nor abroad.
- Must be actively looking for work.
- Must register for the benefit from the National Employment Service.
- Must complete training opportunities.
- This is a one-time benefit.

For more information, including documents required and where to apply: www.segurodedesempleo.cdmx.gob.mx

Main office in Mexico City:
Calle Xocongo 58, Tránsito, 06820 Ciudad de México, segurodedesempleo@cdmx.gob.mx | (57) 09-32-33 Exts. 2010-2014.

Unemployment Benefits for Formerly-employed Private Sector Workers, Mexican Social Security Institute (IMSS)

Have you ever had a job with IMSS benefits and a pension? You may be able to access your pension funds. Normally, you have to wait until you are 60 years old and have worked for 500 weeks to get these funds. But if you are unemployed, you can get a maximum of 30 days' worth of savings from your account once every 5 years. But remember, this means you will have less money for your retirement. For more information on this option visit: https://www.gob.mx/consar/articulos/retiro-parcial-por-desempleo-239845?idiom=es

To apply, visit your local IMSS office: http://www.imss.gob.mx/directorio

Building A Career

Some people want to have a career. A career is a particular line of work that they can grow within and enjoy. Building a career takes time and planning. But it can be worth it. If you build a career you get to do work you are interested in.

What am I good at?
Knowing your strengths and weaknesses is an important first step toward a career. Start by listing these on paper. This will take some time and concentration. Feel free to ask people who know you well for help with figuring out your abilities and shortfalls.

What do I know how to do?
Take some time to think about your work experience. This includes volunteering, mentoring, and taking care of family members. Include anything that had an impact on you, or anything that helped you learn something.

What is out there?
Which parts of the economy are growing, and which are shrinking? Where are the best opportunities and the biggest needs? How do your skills line up with what your community needs? What about the larger society?

What do I want to do?
You have written down what you are good at and the work you have done in the past. You've looked at what jobs are out there. Now you are ready to think about actual careers. Consider the following questions:

- Where do you see yourself in five years?
- What is your dream job?
- What kind of work would you be happy doing for the next 10 years?
- Do you want to work with people, food, or animals?
- Do you seek factory work, a desk job, or work done entirely on a computer?
- Are you drawn to building things, serving people, or creative jobs?

Building Experience

To start your career you need to match your skills and interests with real jobs. You may not currently have a lot of experience in the career you want. That does not mean you can't achieve your dreams. You have some options.

- **Volunteer or intern with an organization part time.** Volunteer positions and internships are a good way to build experience and contacts. Search online for opportunities and talk to people you know. Look on bulletin boards in libraries and other community venues. Volunteering can help you get a job and make you feel good as a person. See the Voting and Engaging with Your Community section and the Directory.
- **Seek higher education.** Some jobs require college degrees. Job listings almost always say if a certain degree is required or preferred. Being a student can be rewarding. It can be a change of pace from full-time employment. In Mexico, college is easier to attend and less expensive than in the US.
- **Start your own organization or business.** As we discussed above, starting your own business can help you build a good career. This is a hard choice, but it can make you happy. It takes a lot of perseverance and imagination, but you will be proud one day to say you started your own business! If you want to start a business, think about what your community needs and wants. Talk to other small business owners for advice.
- **Be realistic.** Not everyone gets their dream job. Still, a lot of people end up doing things they enjoy. Plan ahead and be realistic. Some careers take more time and money than others to achieve, and some take many tries to break into. Don't be afraid to fail a few times.

"To start your own business in Mexico you need drive and you need patience. It's also important to invest in good security for your place of business. After starting my laundry in Puebla, Mexico, it was a year before I saw any profits. You have to be prepared for that."
—Oscar S.

Education

Think about going back to school after you are deported. Education is good for the mind. It introduces us to new people and ideas and helps us understand the world. This guide is made by the University of Illinois at Urbana-Champaign, so of course we are strong supporters of education!

Think of yourself as a lifetime learner. Take classes when you are working and after you retire. Sometimes you will take a class to get better jobs. At other times you'll take a class for fun. You may take a class to explore a new kind of job. You can be in school part-time or full-time. Explore the options in your community.

This chapter covers the following topics:

- Adult education and courses
- Vocational training
- Transferring credits from US schools
- Higher education

Adult Education

Did you finish your elementary school? What about high school? If not, this is a good place to start. Many jobs require this basic education.

Where to get help. Contact your local INEA ("National Institute for Adult Education" or "Instituto Nacional para la Educación de los Adultos"). INEA will look at your past studies in the US or in Mexico. They can give you a test to help you sign up for the right course. INEA also offers literacy courses for teenagers and adults. For more information, visit: https://www.gob.mx/inea/.

The Secretary of Public Education is in charge of education programs from preschool to university. You can contact them by calling (866) 572-9836 or online at www.mexterior.sep.gob.mx.

English Courses

After living in the US, you may have some knowledge of English. Why not get better? Enroll in an English course. You will have more job options as your English improves.

Where to get training. All major cities have many language schools to choose from (Harmon Hall, Interlingua, and QuickLearning, to name a few). Most small towns have at least one or two. Prices and times vary, so shop around. Your state's "Instituto de Capacitación para el Trabajo," or (ICAT) may have free English classes. (See Vocational Training below.)

Computer Courses

Many jobs require basic computer skills. Mexico X is a government program that has free, online classes that can help you learn about computers. For more information, including a list of courses, visit https://www.mexicox.gob.mx/

Vocational Training

Are you interested in a job in construction, plumbing, auto mechanics, carpentry, or another skilled trade? You may want to do vocational training. Vocational training is education that teaches you to do a specific job or skill. There are many places to get vocational training.

Every state has a job training center. The centers are part of the national "Instituto de Capacitación para el Trabajo," abbreviated ICAT. They have classes in auto mechanics, plumbing, furniture-making, and English. Look online to find the ICAT centers near you. Search for "ICAT" and the name of your city or state. Mexico City's is https://www.icat.cdmx.gob.mx/.

CONALEP ("Colegio Nacional de Educación Profesional Técnica" or National Professional Technical Educational College) offers classes to high school-age students who want to do technical jobs. They have 308 campuses operated by 30 state colleges. For more information, visit: https://www.conalep.edu.mx

Transferring Credits from US Schools

The Mexican government has made it easier to transfer your credits from US schools to schools in Mexico.

1. Go to the school where you or your children plan to attend.
2. Bring copies of birth certificates.
3. Bring report cards and transcripts from the US schools you or your children attended.
4. The school will look at your documents. They will help you transfer credits and put you in the right grade level.

For more information, see this education guide, produced by the Mexican government. https://www.gob.mx/cms/uploads/attachment/file/585025/GU_A_EDUCATIVA_2020_-_V141020_.pdf

Even if you don't have any ID or documents you should be able to get an education. No one should stop you from getting access to school. If you have problems transferring credits, you can contact these organizations:

- Institute for Women in Migration, AC (IMUMI) Tel. (55) 521-4153 and 5658-7384. immumi.org
    - Legal Clinic Tel. (55) 9131-7512 & 9154-8990. Tel. USA (208) 753-7041, Email: contacto@imumi.org
- Otros Dreams en Acción, http://www.odamexico.org

☆ Do you have children in school? You may be able to get a monthly government payment of 800 pesos during the school year. Learn more: https://www.gob.mx/becasbenitojuarez/articulos/beca-bienestar-para-las-familias-de-educacion-basica

College Programs

Do you already have a high school diploma? Or maybe you have a GED or "certificado de bachillerato" as it's called in Mexico. If so, you should think about going to college. College is much cheaper in Mexico than in the US. At public universities, it's almost free. Even the most expensive schools in Mexico are still cheaper than many schools in the US!

Where Should You Apply?

Not all colleges are the same. Think about the location, how big it is, what programs it has, and whether it is public or private. Research colleges online or talk to friends and family. Compare costs. You might want to start by looking into your local public college. For a list of technical schools and universities in Mexico visit: https://en.wikipedia.org/wiki/List_of_universities_in_Mexico

Applying for College

Step 1: Get the Application. Most colleges have online applications on their websites. You can also call the school's admissions office and ask them to send an application to you. Or you can go to the admissions office and pick one up.

Step 2: Gather Your Information. You will probably need your CURP, your INE or other official ID. You will also need the dates you went to high school and college, and unopened transcripts from high school, GED, and/or college.

Step 3: Submit the Application. After submitting the application, you will hear back from colleges from within a few weeks to a few months. If you have questions, contact the school's admissions office.

Step 4: Take the Admissions Exam. Many universities have an entrance exam that is scheduled on a specific day each semester. Check with the school where you are applying.

If you started your degree in the US, you may be able to finish your degree online. You can possibly finish it online at that college or a different one in the US. For instance, the University of Illinois offers 17 online bachelor's degrees.
www.online.uillinois.edu/catalog/OnlineDegrees.asp?DegreeType=bachelors

Keep in mind that you will be paying in dollars, not pesos. You may also have to pay out-of-state or international tuition. Still, a degree from a US university may be in your best interest. Learn more: https://www.affordablecollegesonline.org/college-resource-center/online-degree-completion-programs/

Paying for Your Education

While college is much cheaper in Mexico, there will still be costs. Check to see if you can get scholarships. Compare prices of universities near you. Think about location. Will you need to pay for public transportation to get to your college? Is there a university just down the street?

Financial Aid/Scholarships

Each university or program has ways to help you pay. They may offer different kinds of scholarships and financial aid. For example, the University of Chiapas gives scholarships to students who cannot pay the semester fee. The scholarship is about 1,000-2,000 pesos per semester. It covers transportation and food. Private schools are more expensive but also offer scholarships. For example, Tec de Monterrey in Mexico City offers some 100% scholarships for students. Otros Dreams en Acción in Mexico City offers money to returning citizens who want to transfer their credits to Mexican schools.

There is also a new government scholarship program called SUBES. Learn more and register here: https://www.gob.mx/becasbenitojuarez/articulos/estudiante-de-educacion-superior-estas-interesada-o-interesado-en-alguna-de-nuestras-becas?idiom=es

The Education Justice Project offers scholarships of 10,000 pesos (roughly $600 US) to formerly incarcerated and deported people. We also offer scholarships to people formerly incarcerated in prisons in Mexico. The money can be used for vocational training, secondary and university programs. Scholarships are awarded each spring. For more information write to becas@educationjustice.net

Health

When you return to your home country you will need to think about healthcare. Luckily Mexico has free healthcare that is easy to use.

Start by asking friends and family for recommendations of good doctors and health services. If you return to Mexico you will be eligible for one of three public health systems. It will be your responsibility to sign up, stay on top of appointments, and keep yourself healthy.

In this section, we cover:

- Medical care
- Healthcare plan options
- Private healthcare
- Dental and vision care
- Staying healthy
- Paying for medications
- Mental health and substance abuse
- COVID-19: What you need to know
- HIV/ AIDS

Medical Care

The training to become a doctor in Mexico is not as hard as in the US. Still, there are many good doctors throughout the country. Hospitals are usually modern and well-equipped. State-of-the-art specialist hospitals can be found in Mexico City and other cities.

Seeing a doctor is quite affordable, compared to the US. If you are enrolled in Mexico's universal health care system, INSABI (Institute of Health for Wellbeing) you can go to the doctor for free. You may have to wait, though. Even if you chose to pay out of pocket you won't be hit with a huge bill like in the US. You can see a general practitioner for just 45 pesos or $2.20 USD! To see a specialist, you can expect to pay between $30-$50 USD for a short consultation.

Public Healthcare

There are three government-sponsored healthcare systems in Mexico. If you enroll in one, your medical expenses are free or minimal. How much you pay will depend on which program you are eligible for. The quality of your care can also depend on where you live. It's common to have to wait, unless your issue is life-threatening.

Private Practice

As in the US many doctors have their own private practices. You can call and make an appointment with them as you would in the US. The fee is usually around 500-1,000 pesos for a consultation. Some doctors work at a clinic during the day and hold private hours at night.

Clinics/Labs

There are many small clinics or labs in Mexico. Chopo (chopo.com.mx) is one well-respected lab. They do things differently than you might think. You can walk into most of these clinics and "order up" what you would like. You can order a colonoscopy or blood tests and a physician will do them. You might also have a private doctor who sends you to one of these labs for testing. They may ask for an order (orden médica) from your doctor.

Emergency numbers in Mexico:

- Emergency: 911
- Non emergency police: 060
- Red Cross: 065
- City hotline: 070 (in some cities)
- Information: 040
- Fire department: 068
- Anonymous report (abuse or corruption by a government official): 089
- Highway emergency: 074

Pharmacies

One of the cheapest ways to see a doctor is through a local pharmacy. Most pharmacies have a mini-clinic attached to the building. These pharmacies sometimes have no charge to see the doctor or charge very little, 30 or 50 pesos. These rates are so low because the doctor will probably tell you to take medicine that you will buy at the pharmacy. Be aware of this. Because this is how they make money, doctors sometimes give prescriptions you might not really need.

Hospitals

Mexico has many modern hospitals, both public and private. If you are enrolled in public healthcare you will go to your assigned hospital. What happens if you go to a private hospital but you don't have private insurance? You will have to pay all of the costs yourself. This will be expensive.

Seeing a doctor at a pharmacy is ok for something like a cold or indigestion but if you feel there's something more serious going on, don't take chances! Go to the ER or see a specialist.

—Anya V.

Healthcare Plan Options

Institute of Health for Wellbeing (INSABI)

The Institute of Health for Wellbeing offers a healthcare program for people who don't have other insurance. Anyone in Mexico can use it. A lot of people use it who don't have official jobs or who can't afford private insurance.

The program gives you coverage for:

- Medical
- Surgical
- Pharmacy and medicine
- Hospital services
- Catastrophic coverage. This helps people who have expensive illnesses or who have had bad accidents.

With INSABI you don't have to sign up. All your treatment is free. All you need to do is go to your closest health department (Centro de Salud) with your CURP, birth certificate, and INE.

Mexican Social Security Institute (IMSS)

You can use IMSS if you have a full-time job at a Mexican company. To use it, you have to pay some of your salary each month. With IMSS you get healthcare coverage and it will help you if you have an accident or get sick and can't work. You can use IMSS even if you are a foreign employee with residency status.

What if you don't work for a Mexican company? You can still sign up for IMSS. You will have to pay a monthly fee. You can use IMMS even if you have private insurance.

How to sign up:
If you work full-time for a Mexican company you will be automatically signed up. Your company will take the money out of your paycheck every month.

If you are not formally employed you can begin the application online at https://serviciosdigitales.imss.gob.mx/portal-ciudadano-web-externo/home or in person at your local IMSS office (between 8am and 3:30pm). You'll still need to submit paperwork at your local IMSS office (originals and copies) which includes:

- Application form and health questionnaire provided by IMSS
- Official ID
- Proof of address, e.g. your latest electricity bill
- CURP
- Marriage certificate (if applicable)
- Birth certificate
- Two photographs, same format and rules as those for your ID or residency permit
- Bank payment receipt for the first-year's premium. You should have paid this on the day you visit the local IMSS office.

Price for Voluntary Enrollment

The price for annual enrollment depends on your age. It ranges from 6,850 to 16,450 pesos every year. For the specific charge visit: www.imss.gob.mx/derechoH/segurosalud-familia

Pre Existing Conditions

Pre-existing conditions are illnesses you had before you signed up for insurance. IMSS won't cover some of these.

They don't cover:

- Malignant tumors
- Congenital diseases
- Chronic degenerative diseases
- Addictions
- Mental illness
- HIV
- And others

If you have any of these preexisting conditions, you cannot use IMSS. For some preexisting conditions, you can join the program. But you may have a waiting period before you can get healthcare for your condition.

To see if your preexisting condition is covered visit: www.imss.gob.mx/derechoH/enfermedad-seguros-familia

Institute for Social Security and Services for State Workers (ISSSTE)

ISSSTE gives healthcare to people who work for the government. It also helps people with accidents at work. If you work for the federal government you will be signed up automatically. For a more information on ISSSTE visit: www.gob.mx/issste

A note about public healthcare in Mexico:
INSABI, IMSS and ISSSTE are government-run public healthcare programs that cover millions of people. This means that you may have to wait for treatment. And the treatment you get may disappoint you. If your health problem isn't life-threatening, you may be put on a waiting list. How good your care is depends on where you live. Some patients report good care while others are disappointed. A lot of people need healthcare, so the care might not always meet your expectations.

Private Healthcare

Another option for medical coverage in Mexico is private health insurance. Plans have different prices and will cover different things. Private insurance in Mexico is different from in the US in a couple of ways.

Checkups and prescriptions are usually not covered. Doctors and medicine are usually cheaper than in the US, though. Most affordable private plans cover only serious illness and accidents. Deductibles usually cost more than in the US.

If you have a preexisting condition you may not be able to get private insurance. And there are waiting periods for serious illnesses. For example, let's say you are diagnosed with cancer. You've only had insurance for one year. This means you'll have to wait two more years (3-year waiting period) for your insurance to cover your treatment because cancer has a 3-year waiting period. Other conditions will have different waiting periods.

The cost of private health insurance depends on your age, health, and the deductibles and copays that you choose. An average plan for a 37-year-old man in good health with a $1,500 USD deductible, covering serious illness and accidents, costs around $50 USD a month. (1,000 pesos). You can work with your insurer to find a plan that fits your budget.

Two of the largest private insurance providers are GNP (www.gnp.com.mx) and Metlife (www.metlife.com.mx). They also provide auto, life and homeowner's insurance.

Check on the cost of your treatment before you go to your appointments. Don't wait for the insurance company to send you a bill. Health insurance companies should give you information to help you see how much your treatment will cost. You can always call your insurance company if you have questions.

When you get bills, look over them carefully and ask questions so that you understand them. Health insurance companies and organizations make mistakes. It's important to make sure you understand your bills before you pay them.

It's also a good idea to make sure that the doctor you want to see is in your insurance network. If not, you may have to pay the full cost of the visit.

☆ Get an insurance policy that gets you access to an "assessor." An assessor can help you if your insurance company won't pay for something they should. You can use a broker to help you get insurance with an assessor. BTG Seguros www.btgseguros.com is a broker with a good reputation that offers health insurance policies throughout Mexico.

Dental and Vision Care

If you are in one of Mexico's public health programs (INSABI, IMSS or ISSSTE) you also have dental and vision care. But, the government will only pay for procedures for your teeth and eyes. They do not pay for preventative care. In other words, the government will pay for you to get a cavity filled or a cataract removed, but not for you to get your teeth cleaned or eyes checked. You will need to pay for your own prevention care. Get regular checkups for both your teeth and eyes.

Dental and eye care are cheap in Mexico. But the cost and how good they are will depend on where you live. In some parts of the country, teeth cleaning costs only $250 pesos. In other parts you'll be charged $850 pesos. How good the doctors are will depend on where you go. You might use a low-cost clinic for a cleaning, but go to a better dentist for a root canal, even though it costs more.

Do you wear glasses? You can go to a small local optometrist or a large chain store such as Costco. Eye care will cost more at the big stores. There are non-profit organizations that have low-cost clinics. Here are two based in Mexico City:

Asociación para Evitar la Ceguera en México (APEC)
Mexico City
(55) 1084-1400
apec.org.mx
comunicacion@apec.com.mx

Instituto de Oftalmología Conde de Valenciana, Mexico City, Tlaxcala and Guerrero
(55) 5442-1700
institutodeoftalmologia.org

Staying Healthy

Health insurance plans mostly help you deal with problems after they happen. Many of them only treat very serious emergencies. This means you are responsible for getting regular checkups. These checkups help you stay healthy. Find a general practitioner in your community to see you for annual checkups.

A general practitioner can also:

- Give you a full physical exam
- Order lab work
- Help you renew your prescriptions

You should have a full physical at least once a year. If you were in prison or detained in the US you should get tested for infectious diseases. Get tested for HIV/AIDS, Hepatitis C (HCV), Hepatitis B (HBV) and tuberculosis.

Paying for Medications

Most pharmacies have cheaper medicines than in the US. There is usually a generic option. Generic drugs have the same active ingredients but cost less.

In Mexico, the cheapest pharmacy option is Farmacias Similares.

Routine Exams That Can Keep You Healthy

Age	Men	Women
18-39	Blood pressure, cholesterol, flu shot, syphilis screen, TDAP shot, HPV shot, chlamydia/ gonorrhea, HIV, skin exam	Blood pressure, cholesterol, flu shot, TDAP shot, HPV shot, breast exam, after 21 PAP test, chlamydia/gonorrhea, HIV, skin exam
40-64	Blood pressure, blood sugar, colonoscopy (over 50), stool test, flu shot, shingles shot (over 60), prostate screen (over 50), lung cancer screen (only if you smoke), skin exam	Blood pressure, blood sugar, colonoscopy (over 50), stool test, flu shot, shingles shot (over 60), breast screen, mammogram (over 40), lung cancer screen (only if you smoke), postmenopausal bone screening, PAP smear (over 21), pelvic, HPV, skin exam
65+	Blood pressure, blood sugar, cholesterol, colonoscopy until 75, hearing test, aneurysm screen (if smoker), prostate and lung screening (only if you have risk factors), pneumonia shot x2, skin exam	Blood pressure, blood sugar, cholesterol, colonoscopy until 75, hearing test, mammogram until 75, bone screening, PAP smear until 65, pneumonia shot x2, skin exam

Mental Health and Substance Abuse

Deportation is stressful. Mental health support can help everyone during this time. Even if you do not have a mental health disorder, it may help to talk to someone who can to help you adjust.

Lots of deported people have problems with mental health issues or substance use. If you are struggling, get help from a mental health professional. If you feel like you might hurt yourself or someone else, get help right away. Call the suicide hotline at (525) 510-2550. You can also call 911 or visit an emergency room if you are in crisis.

It's harder to move forward if you don't feel good. When you feel mentally healthy, you will feel more positive and hopeful. It may be easier to manage the struggles of deportation.

A mental health professional can help you:

- Change harmful behaviors or cycles.
- Feel stronger as you face your challenges.
- Help you come up with goals and plans to solve your problems.
- Identify how your ways of thinking change how you feel.

Trauma

Trauma from your deportation can also affect your mental health. Trauma is the emotional response you have during a stressful and life-changing event. It can also come from stress that builds up over time. Trauma is more common than people think. Traumatic events that you had as a child can have effects throughout your life.

If you have gone through trauma, treatment or counseling can help. Counselors can help you understand the effects of trauma on your wellbeing, your emotions, and your behaviors.

Some examples of trauma around immigration, according to the American Psychological Association, are:

- **Before:** Money issues, feelings of failure, fear of deportation, escape from violence, poverty, political oppression, threats or disasters
- **During:** Violence, danger, abandonment/separation, seeing death
- **After:** Money issues, conflict in yourself, conflict with others, stress from adjusting to your new home

Do you think you might need medicine for your mental health? Mental health professionals can help you decide if you need medicine. They can offer treatment for drug and alcohol addictions.

Many states have mental health clinics called "Centros Integral de Salud Mental (CISAME)." These clinics have mental health services for children and adults, and people with autism. For information, look on your state's website. For a general list of mental health services by state, visit www.inprf-cd.gob.mx/sitios/hospitales.html

If you are located in Mexico City visit: https://www.gob.mx/salud/acciones-y-programas/centro-integral-de-salud-mental-ciudad-de-mexico-cisame

In Estado de México, visit: https://salud.edomex.gob.mx/salud/cisame

Health insurance in Mexico doesn't cover mental health services. Pharmacies and hospitals can refer you to a professional but you will have to pay yourself. There are nonprofit organizations all over Mexico that offer mental health services. Below we describe a few of them.

There are also non-profit organizations that give support for different disorders and addictions.

- **Centro de Rehabilitación Volver a Vivir, AC.** https://www.facebook.com/VolveraVivirCdJrz/
- **Cauce Ciudadano, A.C.** https://www.facebook.com/CauceAC/
- **AMAR Chihuahua, A.C.** https://www.facebook.com/amarchihuahua/

☆ The Ramon de la Fuente Muñiz National Institute of Psychiatry has a helpful website: http://www.mentalizarte.com/. It talks about how to deal with anxiety, different types of psychotherapy, and common symptoms of mental illness.

If you are struggling with drug or alcohol addiction, there are support groups you can go to for free, such as Alcoholics Anonymous (aa.org) or Narcotics Anonymous (na.org).

Are you struggling with something else? There may also be support groups in your area for issues like:

- Reentry
- Grief
- Mental health
- Disabilities
- Parenting
- Divorce
- Sexuality
- Other issues

To find a support group in your area, you can do a web search ("grupo de apoyo Ciudad Juárez"). Community centers, libraries, and churches can also help you find the support you need. See the Directory and the Healing and Moving Forward section for more information.

> *"You take a pill for your heart, you can take a pill for your head too. It's normal."*
> **—Grant A.**

COVID-19: What You Need to Know

The COVID-19 pandemic continues to get millions of people sick worldwide. Over a million people have died from COVID-19 in the US, and 334,000 people have died in Mexico. There are now new kinds of COVID-19 that spread quickly.

There is some good news. Most people who get COVID-19 get better on their own. But some people are at risk for bad symptoms. People who are older, and people who have conditions like heart disease, diabetes, and people who are obese are at risk.

The most important things to keep yourself and others healthy are:

- Get a vaccine and booster shots (see below).
- Wear a mask around others, especially if you are indoors.
- Keep your distance from others–six feet is the recommended distance.
- Isolate yourself if you are sick or if you spent time with someone who is sick.
- Wash your hands frequently and practice good hygiene.

If you Get Sick

COVID-19 can look like a lot of different illnesses. The most common symptoms are:

- Fever
- Cough
- Shortness of breath
- Fatigue
- Muscle aches
- For some people it starts with nausea, vomiting and diarrhea.

Some people have no symptoms while others become very sick.

If you have mild symptoms, you can treat it at home, as you would a flu bug. Rest and drink lots of water. Take acetaminophen/Tylenol for the fever and drink a warm tea with honey for a cough.

Emergency warning signs

Get medical care right away if you have:

- Trouble breathing
- Pain or pressure in the chest
- Confusion
- You are too sleepy for someone to wake you

Do you think you might have COVID-19? Do you want to get tested just in case? Check with local labs and clinics to see if they offer testing. How much you pay depends where you live and what clinic you go to. Fees usually go from around 300 to 800 pesos.

Some states in Mexico have websites that list where testing is available. In Mexico City, kiosks all around offer the test for free. You can download an app to get your results. (https://test.covid19.cdmx.gob.mx/) Check with your local public hospital or clinic to see if they offer free testing.

Getting a Vaccine

There is no rule that says you have to get a vaccine or booster. But we recommend you get one. The US government has authorized three vaccines. The Mexican government has authorized 10 vaccines to protect against COVID-19, including the ones authorized in the US: Pfizer/BioNTech, Johnson & Johnson, Moderna.

With some vaccines, you'll need to get a couple of shots or booster shots. For more information on each, including the number of countries that have approved its use, see https://covid19.trackvaccines.org/country/mexico/

Some of the vaccines work better than others. But all of them can help us get COVID-19 under control. You probably won't get to choose which one you get. Any vaccine offers more protection than not getting one at all.

How can I get a vaccine?
In Mexico, people over 5 years old can get vaccinated. Check with your local government to see if pre-registration is required. You can pre-register at http://vacunacovid.gob.mx/wordpress/. For more information on COVID-19 and the vaccine in Mexico see https://coronavirus.gob.mx/. Vaccines are available at no cost in Mexico.

Communications

Phones and computers are necessary in the US and your home country. They are used for work, banking, communicating with family, making appointments, ordering pizza, watching TV shows, paying bills, shopping, applying for jobs, and much more.

If you haven't used these technologies, take time to learn. Ask your family and friends to help. Don't be discouraged! A lot of the technology we use now was invented to make things easier for people.

This short chapter covers a few of the things you need to know about getting a phone and internet coverage in your home country.

Getting a Phone

Just like in the US, you will have a few options for phones:

- Basic cell phones for calling and texting
- Smartphones. Almost everyone has a smartphone.
- Landlines. Landlines are more common in Mexico than in the US. They are the cheapest way to call people locally.

Phone plans have different service options. Usually, the services will cover:

- **Talk:** How many minutes you can talk on the phone each month. Many plans these days have unlimited talk time.
- **Text:** How many text messages you can send each month. Many plans these days have unlimited text.
- **Data:** Data enables your phone to connect to the internet when you don't have access to Wi-Fi.

Here are a few common and affordable cell phone plans:

- AT&T has a plan for 224 pesos a month (about $12 USD). It has calls within your country and international calls and 2G of data. There are also 21-day plans that charge 100 pesos a month and offer unlimited calls.
- Movistar and Unefon have affordable plans.
- You can buy "prepaid" cell phones. You have to recharge these phones when your minutes or data run out.
- Some plans come with phones. Or you can buy a phone and a pre-paid balance (saldo).

☆ **Note:** Do you have a phone from the US? You will need to unlock it to use it in Mexico. You can do this at an electronics shop. It can be expensive. If possible, ask the phone's original owner to unlock it for you in the US through their cell service provider.

Calling in Mexico

To call from the US to Mexico, first dial 011, then 52. To call from Mexico to the US, the code is 001. Once in Mexico you will dial the area code of the number you are calling (two or three digits). For example 55 for Mexico City or 443 for Morelia. Then dial the seven-digit number. For a list of area codes in Mexico see: https://en.wikipedia.org/wiki/Telephone_numbers_in_Mexico

Accessing the Internet

You'll need to find a reliable way of using the internet. If you have a laptop, tablet, or smartphone, you can use the internet in many places. Free wireless internet access is available in restaurants, coffee shops, hotel lobbies, chain stores and even parks! You may have to ask for the Wi-Fi password before you can log on with your device.

Just as in the US, you can buy a plan to get the internet from your home.

Need help learning how to use technology?

- GCF global has a lot of free tutorials about how to use technology. Type this address in your search engine and click on the topic you are struggling with: https://edu.gcfglobal.org/en/topics/ To switch between English and Spanish, click the language in the top right corner.
- Wikihow also has lots of resources to help you figure out how to use technology. Type "wikihow" in your web browser, and then enter your question in the search box at the top of the page.
- Adult education programs near you may give lessons on basic word processing and computer use. More advanced classes may include programming code.

Legal Matters

After returning to your country, you may need a lawyer or to go to court.

Dealing with the courts can be challenging. But there are resources to help you. This section has information on finding free lawyers.

☆ We do not give legal advice. We have done our best to give you good information that will help you save time and understand your options. Hopefully, this will set you out on the right path. However, we are not lawyers. Please get the help of a lawyer if you have any questions.

Pro Bono Assistance

The legal system is confusing and frustrating. It is almost always better to get the help of a lawyer rather than trying to do it yourself. Lawyers understand the law and know how local judges and courtrooms work.

Lawyers are often expensive. But there are lawyers who work pro bono, for free. Many law schools in Mexico offer these services. To find one search for the name of your city or state and key words like "servicios legales" or "pro bono."

For a list of pro bono services that work specifically with deportee cases as well as migrants and refugees in Mexico visit: www.refugeelegalaidinformation.org/mexico-pro-bono-directory

Pro Bono Legal Services in Mexico

Name	Location	Website	Description
Fundación Barra Mexicana	Mexico City	https://fbma.org.mx/	Legal help for most issues, especially human rights
Centro de Acceso a la Justicia	Mexico City	http://caj.itam.mx/Paginas/index.html	Legal help from law students, professors, and professionals in many areas, such as divorce, custody, adoption, wills, etc.
Bufete Jurídico Gratuito Universidad Panamericana	Aguascalientes, Aguascalientes	https://www.up.edu.mx/es/noticias/39246/bufete-juridico-gratuito-al-servicio-del-desarrollo-de-atencion-legal	Legal aid clinic, similar to ones in the US
Centro Mexicano ProBono	Mexico City	https://www.probono.mx/	Free legal services for vulnerable populations
Carlos Slim Foundation	Multiple locations in Mexico and the US	https://accesolatino.org/orientacion-legal/	Legal information for Mexicans on both sides of the border.
Without Borders	Mexico City	https://sinfronteras.org.mx/legal/	Helps migrants in Mexico get documents, file asylum claims, and get a free lawyer

Finances, Credit, and Taxes

If you had a bank account or credit card in the US you know how these financial tools work. There are some differences in Mexico that will be good to know about.

In this section, we cover banking basics and how to open a banking account. Then we cover budgeting, financial planning, and credit. At the end of this section, we go over filing taxes and buying property.

Banking

It's a good idea to open a bank account in Mexico so that you have a safe place to put your money. Some popular banks in Mexico include Banorte, Bancomer, Santander and Citibanamex.

Like in the US, bank accounts in Mexico have online services so you can pay bills, move money, and keep records. Your job can put your paycheck directly into your account. Banks in Mexico can also help you with car or mortgage loans, making a retirement investment plan, and investing in stocks and bonds.

Banks will allow you to set up a checking account to keep your money safe. Some checking accounts have monthly fees while others do not, so make sure you ask about fees.

When you open a checking account, you get a debit card. Cash is used a lot in Mexico. But debit cards can be handy and safer than cash. You can use a debit card to buy things, pay bills, or get cash from your account using ATMs.

Do you have a card from the US? Using cards from the US in Mexico can come with hidden fees. If a family member sends you a card, call the bank to find out about any fees before using it.

☆ Credit unions are trustworthy in the US. But they are not trustworthy in Mexico. Do not use "cajas populares."

Opening a Bank Account
You will need these items to open a bank account:

- Official ID. (INE or passport)
- Proof of address. (utility, water, or phone bill)
- A check or cash to make your first deposit. (Ask the bank about minimum deposit amounts.)

Exchange Rate
The peso is currently weak. At the time of publication, the peso is 17 to one dollar. What does this mean for you? It means if you are making pesos you can't buy as much. The prices of many things in Mexico are based on the dollar. The good news is many things are much cheaper than in the US. While making $500 or $1,000 USD a month may sound very low, it will probably be enough if you budget well.

☆ The US dollar sign ($) is often used for pesos. MXN is another abbreviation for pesos.

Financial Resources

You can find a lot of information online about banks, account options, budgeting and strategies for saving your money. Some financial planning websites have a "chat" where you can ask an advisor a question and get an answer right away.

Here are a few US-based sites with information in English:

- NerdWallet is a tool to help you understand banking, credit, and financial planning (www.nerdwallet.com).
- The Simple Dollar is another website with helpful tips about understanding money and budgeting (www.thesimpledollar.com).
- Mint is the TurboTax website that has tools for budgeting and financial management (www.mint.com).

There are good Mexico-based resources available in Spanish as well. Some of these include:

- Coinch is a free app that helps you set savings goals.
- Presupuesto Familiar is an app that lets you organize your debt and spending.
- MisMetasPCC de Pequeño Cerdo Capitalista is an app that helps you set goals and stay on track.

☆ **Disclaimer:** Please remember that we are not endorsing these websites or services. Feel free to do your own looking online.

Avoiding Scams

You don't want to become a victim of a scam. Visit this website for a list of common scams and their warning signs: https://consumer.ftc.gov/articles/how-avoid-scam

Here are a few scams to avoid:

- Be suspicious of emails or calls that offer you lots of money or "free gifts" if you pay a small fee. If the reward sounds too good to be true, avoid it.
- Beware of companies that try to push you into signing up for something immediately. Only sign up for services you understand. You can always ask them for more information if you are confused.
- Only give personal information (such as account numbers and Social Security numbers) to companies you know to be trustworthy.

Credit

In the US, you had a credit score that banks used to decide if they would loan you money. In Mexico, there is no credit score system like in the US. But there is a Credit Bureau (Buro de Crédito) that lets lenders know whether you have good or bad credit. This means you will still want to make sure your credit remains good. Always pay your bills on time. Be aware of services such as TV and internet that come with contracts, often 18 months. If you don't pay for them, they will hurt your credit.

Here are some guidelines for managing credit:

Get educated. The website consumerfinance.gov has helpful information about credit in the US that can also help in Mexico.

Be smart. Avoid businesses (such as car dealerships and payday loan offices) that advertise to people with bad credit. They often have very high interest rates. Do not support any company whose business model depends on your lack of money.

Be cautious. Read the fine print carefully and understand the rules before you sign anything. Remember, what counts is what is in the contract, not what the salesperson promised.

Pay your debts. If you've gotten behind on any of your debts — or have had debts fall into collections — pay them, or make a plan to pay them. See this website: https://consumer.ftc.gov/articles/coping-debt

Pay your bills on time. Paying on time is a good habit and can improve your credit score. The easiest way to do that is by setting up an automatic payment with your bank on your bills' due dates. Marking the dates on a calendar is fine, too.

Use credit cards wisely. If you choose to have a credit card, only charge what you can pay back at the end of the month. If you must borrow money with a credit card to pay your credit card bills, talk with a credit counselor. Don't cosign loans without reading them.

Tax Basics

Once you start earning money you have to start paying taxes. You do this through your RFC number. The amount you pay in taxes depends on how much money you make. It also depends on how much you pay for healthcare and if you have any work-related expenses.

When you file taxes, you let the government know how much you made and how much you have paid in taxes. You also tell them some information about yourself, like whether you have children, how much you pay for healthcare, and if you have a disability. The government decides if you paid too much or too little in taxes. If you have paid too little, you have to pay the amount you owe. If you do not file your taxes, you have to pay a fee and you will owe back taxes for the money you didn't pay. The government can even freeze your bank accounts.

In Mexico, taxes are due every month. Some employers will do this for you. But in other jobs you have to do it yourself. You will need to make an appointment with the tax office to file your taxes (The SAT). There is also a yearly tax return that you have to file. This happens every April.

When you take a job it's important to understand if your company will do your taxes or if you need to do them. Most of the time, they will do taxes for full-time employees. They don't do taxes for freelancers who work for "honorarios" in Mexico.

If you are freelance you have to present your taxes every month to the "Servicio de Administración Tributaria," or SAT. The SAT is the Mexican version of the IRS. The company you work for will ask you for a "factura." The factura will show that you reported your income to the government.

Because the process is confusing, many people hire an accountant. You can hire one for about 500 pesos per month. Ask friends and family if they know a good one. If you don't hire an accountant, you can present your declaration in person each month. It's a good idea to make an appointment online before going. To do so visit https://citas.sat.gob.mx/citasat/home.aspx

☆ Are you supposed to get a tax refund? The government may not give it to you. Make sure you pay only what you owe each month. An accountant can help with this.

Property

Transfer of property can be difficult in Mexico. It is best to use a notary public or lawyer. Note that a notary public in the US is very different from one in Mexico. In the US, notary publics seal and sign important documents. In Mexico, they are like lawyers. They help their clients with policies and procedures. If you need to transfer property a notary public or lawyer will let you know what you need. For a fee they will take care of it for you. They can even help you deal with any back taxes owed.

☆ Some lawyers also can help you title a property. Sometimes they work with a notary, and you'll have to pay the notary fees too. It's sometimes faster to choose a lawyer, even though it may cost more. Whether you choose a lawyer or a notary, be sure to ask for the costs up front. That way they can't surprise you with extra fees.

Voting and Engaging with your Community

Voting

In Mexico, you have the right to vote after deportation, no matter what. And you should! Your voice matters.

And the best news is you don't have to register to vote! You simply show your INE to vote. Your INE is your national ID card.

Take time to understand the issues and the candidates before you vote. Newspapers and candidate websites can help you be informed. Don't forget to vote in local and state elections. Your local and state leaders impact things in your community every day.

For more information on political parties in Mexico see: https://www.bakerinstitute.org/political-parties-mexico/

Quick facts about presidential elections in Mexico:

- The Mexican president serves a term of six years and cannot be reelected.
- The presidential election takes place on the first Sunday of July.
- Inauguration day is December 1.

☆ Did you move to a different state before a presidential election? If your INE says a different state, you'll need to vote in a "Casilla Especial." These are special booths for people from out of state to vote. Find yours at https://computosrm2022.ine.mx/votos-distrito/grafica.

> *Get involved in advocacy work. If we want to change the process, we have to lead the process.*
>
> **—Marlon C.**

Community Organizing

Community organizing is when people join together to stand up for their needs and rights. Community organizing can take many forms, such as going door-to-door to speak to people, or organizing community meetings and fundraisers.

Community organizing can be a good way to make a difference. You would be surprised by what you can do when you work with others!

Community organizations do work online and on the ground. Find an organization and attend a meeting, or start one yourself. Discuss problems that your community is facing and work to solve them.

Volunteer

Volunteer work gives you the chance to meet new people, solve problems and help your community. Volunteering is good for your health, too! Meeting new people can fight depression and make you feel less lonely.

Are you out of work? Volunteering can also help you learn new skills to put on your resume. You may also meet new people who can help you find job opportunities.

Interested in volunteering? You can find opportunities at:

- Schools
- Churches
- Shelters
- Soup kitchens
- Community centers
- Nursing homes
- Animal shelters

Call or visit them to ask how you can help out. You can also do a Google search for volunteer opportunities in your community.

For more information on how to get involved in your community see the Beginning to Heal chapter.

Here's a list of community organizations in Mexico whose members advocate for recently deported people. Get involved!

Name	**Contact info**	**Location**	**Description**
Otros Dreams en Acción	www.odamexico.org	Mexico City	A community of people born in Mexico who grew up in the US and are now back in Mexico because of deportation. Members of ODA help each other with deportation and give each other support.
New Comienzos	www.newcomienzos.org Plaza de la República #9, Tabacalera, Cuauhtémoc, 06030 (55) 7733-1436	Mexico City	Supports people returning to Mexico. They give mental health support, shelter, English certification, mentoring and job search help, youth programming.
Dreamers Moms	https://www.facebook.com/DREAMersMoms (754) 300-8580	Tijuana	Provide support for deported and migrant women and children. They offer food, support and help with housing and jobs. They also have a legal firm, Unión Law, that helps women reunite with families.
Rhizome Center for Migrants	www.rhizomecenter.org	Houston, Guadalajara	They help deported people with legal issues and reintegration into Mexican society.
Comunidad en Retorno	https://www.comunidadenretorno.com/		Collective organization run by deported people. They defend the human rights of deported people and provide a network of support for reintegration.
Deportados Unidos en la Lucha	https://deportadosunidosenlalucha.mx/	Mexico City and virtually throughout Mexico	Help people get their IDS and documents and sign up for government programs. Referrals to other organizations.

☆ For more information about volunteer opportunities in Mexico check out this list of non-governmental organizations in the country: https://catedraunescodh.unam.mx/catedra/catedra/ongmexico.html

Cultural Encounters

If you haven't been to your home country in many years, you may experience culture shock. There are many things that are different between the US and Mexico! It can take a while to get used to these differences. You might have some embarrassing encounters as you learn. Once you have lived there for a while, you may find that there are many things about the culture in your home country that you enjoy.

This chapter contains a few of the things that you should be aware of, such as culture and safety concerns. It focuses on Mexico, though many things are similar in other parts of Latin America.

Greetings

In Mexico, people greet each other warmly. This is especially true in small towns. Make sure you greet people. If you don't, people may think you are cold or rude. It is polite to greet everyone at small parties like a family barbecue. When you leave the party you should say goodbye in the same way to everyone.

- Men greet each other with handshakes.
- Women are greeted with a kiss on the cheek or hug. This is an "air kiss," touching right cheeks and making a kissing sound into the air. This may feel strange at first. You can choose a handshake instead.
- Older women may expect a handshake rather than a kiss.
- Close friends and family members greet each other with hugs, as in the US.
- Handshakes are the norm in the corporate world.

Be nice and courteous to people you see around town. Most people greet each other with "good morning" or "good afternoon" before getting down to business. Most people know their local grocer or store-owner. They greet each other and are courteous to one another.

☆ To stay safe during the pandemic, you may not want to give people kisses, hugs and handshakes. A wave or a fist bump should be fine.

Formality

Mexicans are formal with people they don't know. They call strangers ma'am or sir (señora or señorita for younger women, and señor for men). You'll also hear "Don" or "Doña" for older people. "Joven" might be used to greet younger people. They will call strangers "usted" rather than the more casual "tú." If someone tells you to call them "tú," you should follow their lead.

In Central America, "usted" is often used with spouses and children. "Vos" or "tu" is used for peers and siblings.

Body Language

Eye contact is not as common as it is in the US. It also depends on social classes. Don't be surprised if people tend to look down and avoid eye contact. For some people in Mexico this behavior is a sign of respect. You may also notice that people stand closer to you to talk than in the US.

Punctuality

Mexican society moves a bit slower than it does in the US. People don't get to parties on time. Most people will get to a party an hour late or more. Most people expect you to be on time for appointments and meetings, though some people might be late to meet you.

Bureaucracy

Mexico runs on a slower clock than the US. Getting things done seems to take much longer. You may wait in line at the bank for half an hour or more. When you get to the counter, the worker may pause to answer a phone call or to greet a colleague.

Things like applying for your ID or getting a passport can take a long time. You may have to go back to the agency a couple times and wait for a few hours. You may want to make an appointment online. This can make it go faster. Always visit the government office's website to check the list of documents you need before showing up.

Religion

Religion, especially Catholicism, is important in Mexico and plays a big role in daily life. After all, 85% of the population is Catholic. Many community events, even ones like high school graduations, are celebrated with a mass. The next biggest group is Evangelical Christians. They are less than 2% of the population.

Family

Families in Mexico are typically more tight-knit than they are in the US. Mexicans live near family. They also live at home for much longer than people in the US. For many, family comes before anything else. Parents, grandparents, and kids spend a lot of time together. Respect for older people is an important value. Sunday is often a special day set aside for family.

Friends

Friendships are very important in Mexico and people put a lot of effort into maintaining them. In fact, Mexican culture has "godparents" that make close friends almost like family. If you are close to someone they may ask you to be godparents for their children. As a godparent, you may have to do special things at baptisms, first communion, confirmation, or even a wedding. Being a godparent is an honor. It is also serious. It may cost money as well. You may have to help pay for at least part of a celebration.

Animals

Often, visitors from the US are shocked and saddened by how animals are treated in Mexico. 70% of all dogs live on the street. Many are in bad shape. You'll see animals heading to the slaughter house in the back of trucks. Many pet owners feed their animals table scraps and don't take them to the vet.

There is a growing animal rights movement in Mexico. Dog fighting was outlawed in 2017. Some states have laws against cock fighting. There's even a bill in congress to ban testing makeup on animals.

If you decide to adopt a dog or cat, get them fixed. Local animal welfare groups can help with low-cost options. Ask them for a low-cost vet recommendation.

Safety

You may be worried about your safety in Mexico. As in the US, there are places that are safer than others. Be cautious and use good judgment about where you go and what you carry with you. Here are a few things to be aware of.

Kidnapping

Mexico does have a problem with kidnapping. Don't wear flashy jewelry or show off your wealth. Many people avoid walking at night as well. Kidnappers want to get money. "Express kidnapping" happens when the kidnappers force someone to get money from an ATM.

Be aware of "fake kidnapping" scams. You might get a call from someone who says they have your loved one. They'll ask you to pay them to get your loved one back. Before you pay, contact your loved one to see if they are ok. We suggest you hang up on this kind of call right away and block the number.

Femicide

Femicide is the killing of women or girls. Often, they are killed by family members or spouses and partners. But it can also mean any killing related to gender. In Mexico and Central America, this is a serious problem. In Mexico about 1,000 women and girls are victims of femicide each year. This number is going up. El Salvador has one of the highest rates of murder of women in the world.

Political Violence and Corruption

Political violence is a big problem in Mexico. In the 2021 midterm elections, 89 politicians were murdered. Journalists and environmentalists are also killed.

Government corruption at all levels is another big problem. If you get pulled over by the police they may make up a lie about something you did wrong. They may even threaten to take your car away. They are only supposed to take your car away if you are dangerous, like if you are driving drunk. Sadly, it's normal to give them a bribe, called a "mordida." It's up to you whether you want to do this, of course.

You can call 089 to anonymously report any illegal or corrupt behavior on the part of a government official.

Part 3:
Healing and Moving Forward

- Beginning to Heal
- Mindfulness
- Building Healthy Relationships

Beginning to Heal

Deportation hurts in a lot of ways. Being arrested, detained, and deported can cause trauma. This chapter explores ways you can heal from this trauma, move forward, and become more resilient.

Resilience means that when something bad happens (like deportation), you can bounce back from it. It means that you can cope with stress instead of getting stuck with your bad feelings.

Resilience is something you can learn! It is not something that only some people have.
It is something that everyone can strengthen, like when you build muscle. It takes time and work, but it can be done.

Having resilience doesn't mean stress is easy. It means that you have taught yourself to deal with tough things. Resilience means you have behaviors, thoughts, and actions that help you deal with stress. It means that your difficulties can help you grow.

If you feel stuck, get help from a mental health professional. Getting help is an important part of building resilience.

There are four main areas of resilience. To heal from the trauma of deportation, work to improve your resilience in these four areas.

Build Your Connections

Connect with people you trust and who understand you. Remind yourself that you are not alone. Deportation is a time when you will strengthen old relationships and build new ones. The Relationships chapter can help you with this.

Support groups can help you meet people going through the same things as you. Support groups are available for:

- Drug or alcohol addiction. See Alcoholics Anonymous (aa.org.mx) or Narcotics Anonymous (na.org).
- Deportation
- Grief
- Mental health
- Disabilities
- Parenting
- Divorce
- Sexuality
- Weight loss

Go to your first meeting with an open mind. Listen and learn. Go to a couple of meetings to see if you like the group. If you don't like it, try to find another.

Finding support groups can be tricky, especially if you live in a rural area. The easiest way to find one is through an internet search. You can search terms like:

- "Deported or returned people"
- "Substance abuse support groups"
- "Community support group + name of your community"

Health care providers, community centers, and churches are also good sources of information.

No support groups near you? Join an online support group.

Reach out to somebody. One of our coping mechanisms is to retract ourselves, isolate ourselves to try to deal with what we're going through.

—Pablo M.

If you feel lonely and isolated, get involved in your community to make new friends. Here are a few ideas:

- **Community Organizing, Advocacy, Mentoring, and Volunteering.** Your skills are useful. You can make a real difference by using your skills to help people.
- **Join or Create a Shared Interest Group.** Join a sports team, book club, hobby group, parents support group, or become involved with local politics. You can even organize your own group! Your local public library is a good place to find or post notices.
- **Join a Community Association.** They organize events, like block parties, potluck meals, and musical events. Search online for "community organization + name of your community" or "advocacy group + name of your community." Facebook and other social media apps can help you find groups.
- **Join a Religious Organization.** Join a church, synagogue, or other faith community. They can help you find meaning, purpose, and fellowship. It may take a while for you to find the place that feels right for you. Don't be discouraged. It's okay to go slow.

Foster Wellness

Take care of your body. Your body needs good food, sleep, water, and exercise. All of these things can help it fight stress. Consider finding a gym, jogging, walking, biking, practicing yoga, or looking up free at-home exercise videos online. Practice safe sex by using condoms.

Practice mindfulness. Mindfulness means being present in the moment. You can practice mindfulness in many ways. See the Mindfulness chapter to learn more.

Avoid negative outlets. Stress can make you want to feel better right away. It may make you want to use drugs and alcohol, or other negative things. This is like putting a Band-Aid on a large wound. It won't help you heal. Try to do healthy things to help you cope.

Spend time in nature. Nature can be healing. Grow vegetables in a garden or visit a local park or forest.

Working out and staying into sports was a way for me to stay healthy and motivated. It gave me physical health but also mental stability. It helped me cope with the anxiety of starting all over again. I say all the time, going to the gym and working out is much more than just doing exercise. Being fit gives you confidence and builds self-esteem. Being able to endure difficult things like lifting your max or running to the limit of your capacity builds courage and helps prepare you mentally for those difficult experiences you'll have in life, to keep pushing forward. And eating healthy and staying within your weight limits is also important for living a long productive life.

—Israel P.

Find Purpose

Help others. Helping others can help you feel useful. Get involved with a community organization or help a friend who is struggling.

Invest in what you do. Your job may not be perfect, but how you do it is entirely up to you. What are your strengths? Bring those to your work. Find ways to do a little extra and try new things. Realize the value of the work you do, and honor that.

Be proactive. Ask yourself, "What can I do about this problem?" Set goals for yourself. Break them down into smaller steps. Work towards them, a little each day. The small steps you take will help you keep going.

Learn about yourself. How did deportation help you grow? How have you become a better person? This can help you feel better about yourself.

Learn new things. Be open to new ideas. Pick up a few books or take a class to learn something new. Challenge yourself. Expand your knowledge and thinking.

"*Take care of yourself and everything else will fall into place... You can't stress out over everything that you have no control over. Don't give up hope. There's always hope. And love overcomes a lot of stuff.*"

—Heather B.

Embrace Healthy Thoughts

Keep things in perspective. You can't always control what happens to you. But you do have control of how you respond to the things that happen. Put away negative thoughts. Focus on having more balanced and realistic thoughts.

Accept change. Change is a part of life. Some change might get in the way of your goals. It is ok to accept some things. Focus on the things that you can change and control.

Stay hopeful. No one feels positive all the time. Let yourself feel upset or disappointed for a little bit. Then focus on what gives you hope. What helps you feel positive? What do you want and how can you make that happen?

Learn from your past. Look back at what has helped you in the past during hard times. Remind yourself of how you found strength before. What have you learned about yourself from your past?

Find healthy ways to deal with difficult emotions. You may feel grief, anger, or depression because of what you have gone through. These feelings are natural. Be aware of your good or bad feelings and accept them. Find ways to express them in healthy ways. It is okay to get professional help. Counseling can help you learn to be emotionally well.

We tend to have difficulty finding our footing. We have a purpose, but now it is no longer as clear cut as it once was. Moreover, rather than dealing with the trauma, we tend to ignore it or downplay it as if it is completely normal what we just went through. Before anything, we must deal with our trauma. It is not going away magically. We can do it by asking for help, venting, or riding a bicycle for hours, as I love to do. But we have to address it.

—Roberto L.

Mindfulness

Mindfulness can help you deal with the stress of deportation. This chapter covers the following topics:

- What is mindfulness?
- What are the benefits of mindfulness?
- How do I meditate?
- Meditation scripts
- Meditation resources
- Meditation groups

What is Mindfulness?

Mindfulness is about paying attention to the present. It is about noticing your thoughts, emotions, and how your body feels. It's about not judging yourself or giving yourself a hard time. When you are aware of your five senses or your mind, you are being mindful!

Mindfulness is not about fixing what is wrong with you. Instead, it is about accepting what is going on inside you. It's about being gentle and kind to yourself. It helps us stay connected to the moment. We can then respond in healthy, caring ways.

Mindfulness has its roots in Buddhism, but it is not a religion for most people. Instead, it is a way to explore your mind and body. Some people see mindfulness in every religion. Prayer can be a form of mindfulness.

”

Does your heart race every time you step out of your house or enter a public place? Practicing mindfulness helped me be aware of physically overwhelming experiences at the onset. I could feel perspiration on my upper lip. My palms start getting sweaty. My body tenses up. These are the warning signs that remind me to just breathe. During these episodes, I found that I was not breathing. Doing nothing else but concentrating on my breathing made this experience bearable. Soon thereafter, I was more and more in control.

—Mindfulness Program Participant

What are the Benefits of Mindfulness?

Mindfulness has many benefits. It can help you manage stress and control your emotions. It can even change how your brain works. It can help you not get stuck in bad thoughts. It can help you be happier.

Other benefits include:

- Better able to fight disease
- Lower blood pressure and heart rate
- Better mental focus
- Better handle of emotions
- Lower anxiety and depression
- More growth after trauma
- More self-compassion
- Less burnout

> *Have you felt alone, out of place? You are not alone. I experience that regularly. No one seems to understand what I am experiencing. I rely on mindfulness to assist me in channeling my focus. I do so by simply concentrating on the breath. This simple act is what grounds me and allows me to function normally.*
>
> **—Anonymous**

How do I Meditate?

Meditation is a common way to practice mindfulness.

No training is needed to meditate! There is no one right way to meditate. There is no "good" way, and certainly no "bad" way. If you can breathe, you can meditate.

Practice alone or with a group. Find someone who knows how to meditate to help you get started. You can meditate alone or with a group.

When to practice. In the beginning, try to meditate for 5 or 10 minutes. Make that time longer bit by bit. Try different times of the day: morning, evening, or afternoon. Try to practice every day. But, if something comes up, that's OK! Let go of what you think should happen.

How to sit. Many people meditate sitting down with their eyes closed or open. Sit in a chair or cross-legged on a pillow, floor, or bed. Sit up straight, but be relaxed. Rest your hands in your lap or on your legs.

Common Difficulties. It's normal to feel restless, bored, and sleepy. Your mind may wander. That's totally okay. You don't need to get rid of thoughts when you are meditating. Do your best to notice your thoughts. Label them as they come. You might label them things like "thinking about the past," "feeling restless," or "feeling bored." Then, see if you can bring your attention to your breathing. Meditation takes practice. Do your best to be curious. No matter what happens, try not to judge yourself.

Meditation and Trauma. Sometimes meditation makes you remember things. It may dig up traumatic memories. This may make you feel stressed or anxious. Meditation can help you deal with these feelings. But, it is not a cure-all. If focusing on your body brings up traumatic memories, try focusing on a safe image or sound. If difficult memories keep coming, talk with a mental health professional. Look for a meditation group for people who have trauma.

Meditation Scripts

Many begin their meditation journey by using meditation scripts, or words they can read or listen to while meditating. Read each script slowly to get used to it. After a while, you can say the words silently to yourself. Give each step about 1 minute, but feel free to go at your own pace.

> *I don't always follow a specific regimen other than just to breathe in times of stress. This sounds simple enough but it can be very difficult, especially when you are not practicing regularly.*
>
> **—Anonymous**

A Seated Breath and Body Meditation Practice | Abbreviated from Mindful Magazine

1. Begin by getting comfortable, sitting up straight but not rigid, in a position of ease. Close your eyes or lower your gaze toward the floor.
2. Take a few deep breaths. Get a sense of how you're doing at this moment physically, emotionally, and mentally. Is there tension or tightness anywhere? Is your mind busy or calm?
3. As you breathe in, bring a beginner's mind, noticing things for the first time. As you breathe out, bring the same sense. Rest your awareness on the breath.
4. Begin to sense your body sitting here. Feel into your whole body. What are your senses telling you? You may feel warm or cold. You may be itchy. Perhaps some areas don't have any feeling at all – a blank. Spend the next minute feeling these sensations. Allow them to come and go.
5. If your mind wanders, where is it wandering to? Are you remembering something? Are you feeling anger or regret? Are you practicing what you will say to someone? Notice your thoughts as if you were sitting in a movie theater, watching images come and go on the screen. Notice the thought or emotion as if it were someone else's thought, not yours. Notice an opening up in yourself as you become more aware, more accepting.
6. Come back to the breath. Breathe in and out. Notice how the whole body expands when you inhale, and contracts when you exhale. The whole body is breathing.
7. As you end, congratulate yourself for taking time to meditate. Realize that you can take a few minutes to meditate whenever you wish.

> *"Have you experienced disappointment? I have and that is not something to be ashamed of. I constantly ruminate on these disappointments. Rumination occurs naturally when you allow your mind to take control. Mindfulness has taught me how to take control of my thought process. This has allowed me the freedom to take life as it comes and adjust as needed."*
>
> **—Anonymous**

Gratitude Meditation | Mindvalley Academy

Gratitude practice can help us tap into hope. It can help us boost our mood. That said, it's not easy to focus on the positive when you feel stressed. Be patient with yourself as you try this meditation. You can always return to the breath if it feels too stressful.

1. Sit in a comfortable position. Take a few deep and slow breaths.
2. Think about something that's troubling you. It's best to start small. Name something that annoys you. Perhaps the room you're in is cold and drafty.
3. Now see if you can flip it to something positive. For example, perhaps the room is cold and drafty, but it's raining and you're able to stay dry.
4. Continue to think of things or experiences that you don't like. Do your best to find something positive about each thing or experience. Challenge yourself. Maybe they are helping you learn or grow. Perhaps you notice how you have kept going even when things are hard. Maybe you have found new ideas you didn't have before.
5. You can also simply repeat, "I am grateful for ______" and notice what comes up.

Mindful Walking | Adapted from Mindful Walking, Segal, Williams & Teasdale Mindfulness-Based Cognitive Therapy for Depression

Mindfulness is about being aware of what we're doing, thinking, and feeling. Mindful walking is simple. You can do it without people knowing what you're doing. Many people walk everyday, but most of us don't focus on the process of walking and how the body feels.

1. Standing still, become aware of your feet. How do your feet feel when they touch the ground? Flex your knees a few times to get a sense of how your feet and legs feel.
2. When you start walking, notice how you move your weight into each leg. One leg "empties" and the other leg takes over to support your body
3. With one leg "empty," allow the other heel to rise slowly. Move it forward, feeling your leg. Place it down to get ready for the next step. Feel your weight move to this leg.
4. Continue walking. Notice how your feet, legs, hips, and upper body feel.
5. If you stop, notice how you feel when you stand. Notice how it feels when you start moving again.

Mindfulness Resources

Need more meditations? Check out this website for more meditation scripts! https://drive.google.com/file/d/1XSgYgKhvpM1ugq3_0OQ074nBXlZq4CLo/view?usp=sharing

Phone apps. There are lots of free mindfulness phone apps. These apps offer:

- Guided meditations
- Timers
- Calming sounds
- Soothing voices
- Tips on how to sleep better or be less anxious

You can use these apps on the bus or train, at work, or before bed. You can choose long or short meditations. Some popular apps include Aura, Calm, Headspace, Insight Timer, Mindfulness Coach and UCLA Mindful. Do an online search for more information on these apps.

> *"Remind yourself that the deepest stillness and peace does not arise because the world is still or the mind is quiet. Stillness is nourished when we allow the world, the mind, and the body to be just as they are for now, moment by moment, and breath by breath."*
>
> **—Williams & Penman, Mindfulness**

Meditation Groups

Meditation groups are great ways to meet people and practice. If you are a beginner, they can help you learn. They can help you keep going when you feel like quitting. Some are face-to-face while others are online. Many groups begin with a few friends meeting in someone's home.

Tergar.org. Tergar is an international meditation community. It has a program for beginners who want to start meditating. The program is called "The Joy of Living" and is based on the book by the same name. Tergar has meditation communities all over the world, including ones in Mexico City and Puebla, Mexico. It also has online classes, meditation practice materials, and more. There is also a website in Spanish: espanol.tergar.org

Some meditation groups may say they are Buddhist. They may use words like "Sangha" (community), "Zen" (meditative state), or "Vipassana" (insight). You may not have to be Buddhist to join. Many groups are open to anyone joining their group. Some mindfulness groups also focus on mental health. They can help you reduce pain or deal with stress and anxiety.

> *"It is common to question your purpose. I do so repeatedly. My relationships aren't exactly as I had envisioned. Mindfulness meditation provided me the space and compassion to accept people as they come. I learned to let the little things go and focus on what makes that person special to me."*
>
> **—Mindfulness Program Participant**

Building Healthy Relationships

Relationships are always hard. Detention and deportation make them even harder. If you have been deported, you might have left family behind in the US. We know how painful this separation can be. Staying connected with family who are far away is hard.

Maybe you have reunited with other family and friends in your home country.
This can bring challenges, too. Reconnecting with them and building healthy relationships takes patience and care.

Maybe you have been away from your home country for a long time. Now you have to start over and make new friends. This can also be hard.

There is no one-size-fits-all solution to the relationship challenges you may face. This section has words of advice from people who have gone through deportation.

This chapter covers the following topics:

- Staying close when you're far away
- Rebuilding old relationships
- Forming new relationships
- Dealing with difficult emotions
- Domestic violence

Staying Close When You're Far Away

Detention and deportation strain relationships. For a lot of people this is the hardest part of deportation. The separation is hard for both you and your loved ones.

Try to keep up communication through letters and phone calls, when possible.

> *It's hard, but you have to make your kids understand that you don't want to be away from them... You love them and you're going to do everything you can to make sure you're in their life.*
>
> **—Tony C.**

During the deportation process your relationships will change. Some may end, and all of them will face challenges. Some people find it so hard they distance themselves from their loved ones.

> *You don't want to worry your family with those issues. You get on the phone, and you grind your teeth. Regardless of what you're feeling, you're going to tell them that everything is going to be OK. You get in this habit of keeping things bottled up, and you're dealing with some degree of loneliness and emptiness, because you're not sharing it with your family.*
>
> **—Roberto**

You may feel this way, like you want to drift apart from your loved ones. Don't. Stay in touch as much as you can.

Sometimes individuals think that since they're getting deported then they can burn bridges or simply neglect their relationships with their loved ones in the US. Well, the reality is that who better to help you or just lend you an ear than those who have actually been there? People can make friends anywhere in the world. But, to truly attain the emotional stability and freedom that I believe we all seek, then you are going to need people in your life who are aware of your circumstances and who are willing to offer that emotional support. I believe this is something a family can provide and thus the imperative to foster and nourish healthy relationships with your family, even if you are getting deported.

—Roberto

Find other ways to keep in touch. It's hard to be separated from your loved ones. But there are other ways to be present. Talk, listen, and provide support when and how you can. Use technology to stay in touch.

Get up to date on the newest apps that let you stay in touch with your loved ones in the US, such as Skype, WhatsApp, Facetime, and Messenger. Through these apps you can message, have phone calls or video chats and see their faces.

—Erick N.

I take time out of my day, even five minutes, to call them and see what's going on. I text them every day, every morning... I talk to them and get their point of view and see what's going on, try to spend time. I tell them I love them, how you doing, how's your day going, what you got planned. Little simple stuff. I let them talk. You gotta try to be involved, no matter how old they are, they are still children, they still want that relationship with you.

—Tony C.

Relationships are a two-way street. Family members can also do a lot to stay close to loved ones who are deported or detained.

I send him a little bit of money, enough to keep phone calls going, you know, and pictures and stuff and try to set up options for him so he knows he doesn't have to go back to the same stuff. Just let him know that there's help, there's better things in life. I try to talk to him about the good stuff, about working and going to church, when we're playing games with his little sister and stuff like that.

—Heather B.

Rebuilding Old Relationships

Are you going back to your home country? You might feel scared, worried, or excited about reuniting with family and friends who live there. You might have not seen them for many years.

You can get ready by thinking about your relationships. Be honest with yourself. Who will be a good, supportive influence in your life? Be realistic about how life will go after you return. You will all need time to adjust.

Tell your loved ones what you need when you get there. Tell them what you are hoping for. This could include both emotional and financial support. Never be afraid to ask for patience.

Listen to the needs and concerns of your loved ones, too. Reuniting will be easier if you can talk ahead of time and learn to compromise.

Keep in mind that you are entering somebody else's space. You must be mindful of the relationships around you.

—Pablo

Maybe you were away for a long time. You'll need to relearn who you are and who your loved ones are. Kids who were young when you left may be much older now. You may have a different idea of your relationship than they do.

> *Don't come in like they're supposed to know you or even respect you a little bit, because you've been gone. You gotta gain that respect and that trust back when you've been gone so long.*
>
> **—Keke**

Think about the ways you have changed. You and your loved ones have both grown. Know that this growth is good. Be open to the person before you and who they are now.

> *Oftentimes when people are anticipating going home, they have ideals and expectations on how their reunification with family will be. There's the dream and there's the reality. It's good to have these great expectations, but don't set yourself up for disappointment if people don't live up to the expectations you have of them.*
>
> **—Joe Joe**

It may be very hard to ask for help from loved ones if you've been away for a while. Pablo notes:

> *I need assistance with the most basic things. That does make me somewhat defensive, and I'll end up trying to do things on my own and then I crash and burn.*

His advice?

> *Ditch that machismo and ask for help. It's not a bad thing.*

Lee, whose partner was deported, says that

> *Healthy adult relationships aren't about putting your needs in the back seat.*

She explains:

> *You want to be considerate and not wear out your welcome. The effect of that is that maybe you're not expressing the things that you need. It's OK to say, 'Hey, I need you to do this thing for me.' Learn to communicate what you need.*

Joe Joe offers this final piece of advice about asking for help:

> *If you strive to lighten someone's load rather than adding to it, they are going to be more receptive to helping you. This is what really wins people over and will help get you where you need to go.*

Forming New Relationships

People who are detained or deported often feel lonely. Isolating yourself might have helped while you were detained or incarcerated.

> *You spend so much time keeping people at arm's distance. You never let anybody get close. You've gotten so used to keeping people at a distance that you just continue to do it. It's hard to make new friends.*
>
> **—Tony C.**

You will need to learn to open up back up to people. Being open will help you build new relationships in your home country.

Self-disclosure is sharing information about ourselves that is truthful. It is being honest with others. It is one of the most important parts of a healthy relationship.

- It builds trust.
- It gives you emotional release.
- When you share, others are more likely to share, too.

There are risks to sharing. You may worry that people will reject you if they know how you feel. You may feel like people won't understand what you have gone through. All this can make you afraid to share.

Remember, getting close to someone doesn't happen overnight. You can choose what to share and when. When building relationships, most people share slowly. They take small steps and wait to see how people respond. Here are some tips for learning to open up to others:

- **Start with the easy stuff.** Share what you like to do for fun. Ask them what they like to do. What movies do they love? What do they do to relax?

- **Spend time together.** Take long walks. As you do, share some of your feelings, fears, and goals. Invite them to open up, too. Start small and see how they respond.
- **Learn to text.** Send short, friendly messages about your day. Ask how they are doing.
- **Try not to criticize or give advice when they share things with you.** Just listen. Be positive and supportive.

> *My approach is to be aware that I have a lot to offer to a friendship. I realize that I don't possess a strong network here in my new city but conversely I also understand my strengths which are a willingness to learn and to work. Moreover, my past is the past. I choose not to allow that to define me as an individual nor my future.*
>
> **—Roberto L.**

Dealing with Difficult Emotions

You probably feel good things toward your loved ones. You may feel things like love, concern, and care. But you also may feel things like guilt, loss, frustration, anger, and grief. Maybe you bottle up tough emotions instead of working through them. Maybe you push aside bad feelings and instead tell loved ones that everything is OK. Your loved ones may do the same.

Here are a few of the emotions you might feel as you figure out relationships after deportation.

- **Fear** is your body's reaction to danger or uncertainty. You may be afraid that your family in your home country won't accept you. This fear can make you pull further away from them.
- **Sadness** is feeling unhappy or discouraged. You might feel discouraged that you are no longer able to see your children every day.
- **Grief** is a feeling of loss. You might feel loss for the years you spent away from your family.
- **Guilt** is feeling bad about yourself. You might feel guilt over something you've done or haven't done that makes others suffer. Maybe you feel guilty for not being around for your partner or kids.
- **Anger** is something you feel when someone or something has done you wrong. You might feel angry about deportation, or angry about something a loved one has said.

People feel their emotions in their mind and body. Fear can tighten your chest. You might feel sick to your stomach or start sweating. Some feelings can help you change and grow. Others can stop you from growing and hurt your relationships.

Emotions that you push down will come out eventually. Sounds, tastes, and smells can bring back memories from the past. You may have lost partners, friends, and parents through deportation. Expect to feel rage, sorrow, frustration, and grief.

> *If you have any emotions at all, you're going to have guilt about making your family suffer. Because you're not suffering alone. They suffer with you. And we don't like to show [our emotions] because, hey, we're tough guys*
>
> **—Tony**

> *I was looking at videos with a friend and a song came on. I found myself crying for no apparent reason. I lost my father when I was locked up. That was one of his favorite songs. I had never had the opportunity to mourn. All of the pain came forward.*
>
> **– Pablo**

It's normal to feel these emotions. It's what you do with these emotions that matters. Pushing them aside instead of facing them can hurt your relationships. Learning to recognize, express, and manage emotions can help you have healthier relationships.

Here are some tips for dealing with emotions in healthier ways:

- **Name your feelings.** Let them wash over you. They won't last forever. Give yourself time to feel them. Don't bury them. Burying them can make these feelings build up even more.
- **Express your feelings in helpful ways.** People are different from their actions. "I'm angry about something you have done," not "I am angry with you."
- **See the difference between feeling and acting.** Just because you feel a certain way doesn't mean you have to act on it.
- **Take responsibility for your feelings.** Try not to blame others for the way you feel. Instead of saying, "You're making me angry," say "I'm feeling angry."
- **Change your view.** Think about what made you feel that way. Are there different ways to think about what happened that are more helpful?

Therapists or counselors can help you deal with your emotions. It may help to go to family or couples therapy.

Domestic Violence

Domestic violence is when one person uses power or control over another person in a dating, family, or household relationship. Domestic violence isn't just an anger problem. It's about control.

There are many kinds of domestic violence:

- Verbal abuse (threats, name-calling, intimidation)
- Physical abuse (pushing, slapping, choking, destroying property)
- Controlling behavior (stopping you from seeing people, going places, or spending money)
- Emotional abuse (making you feel like you are worthless)
- Sexual abuse (unwanted sexual activity, often using force)

In some families or cultures, these behaviors are not seen as wrong. This can make it hard to break away. It may take some time to change your way of thinking. It may take some time to realize that what you are doing or experiencing is wrong.

If you are in an abusive relationship, get help. Deciding to leave can be risky. You may fear for your safety or the safety of your kids. You may need the other person for money. It takes a lot of courage to leave.

You can start by calling a domestic violence hotline. The organization "Origen" offers one for free at (800) 015-1617 or through WhatsApp: (55) 3234-8244. This hotline can give you support, information, and referrals. They can put you in touch with resources in your area. Even if you are not ready to leave the relationship, the hotline can help you get through tough times. They can also help you take the next step. The hotline is confidential, so they will keep your information private.

For more resources for people facing violence at home, visit www.origenac.org

For a list of domestic violence shelters across Mexico, visit https://www.facebook.com/RedNacionaldeRefugiosAC/

If you are the abusive partner

Have you abused your partner or family member? Reach out to get help. The first important step is to admit you have a problem. You can change, but it will take work. You may choose to stay away from your family for a while. This can keep them safe and give them some space.

Think about getting help from a therapist. For some government and nonprofit resources, see the Health chapter.

Part 4:
Deportation to Central America

- Deportation to Central America
- Deportation to Guatemala
- Deportation to Honduras
- Deportation to El Salvador

Deportation to Central America

A lot of the information in this guide so far has been about Mexico. If you're going to Central America, your experiences may be different. The Prepare for Possible Deportation section has advice about what happens before deportation. This includes your rights, how to get legal help, how to create a family plan, and more.

This section has information for people deported to Guatemala, Honduras, and El Salvador. First, you'll learn what happens before deportation. This includes how to plan ahead and what to expect on the day of deportation. It also lists organizations that can help you figure out if you have an asylum case. Then, each section is broken down by country. Each one discusses what you'll face as you return.

Central America tends to be more dangerous than Mexico. It also has fewer resources. If you come from Central America, you may have a stronger asylum claim. The Prepare for Possible Deportation section has more information on claiming asylum.

Finally, Central America's borders are open for citizens. This means you can move freely among Guatemala, Honduras, El Salvador, and Nicaragua. Some deportees have moved after deportation to other countries. But, you will need a visa to do that.

> *My family and I made the decision to relocate to Antigua, Guatemala after my deportation to Honduras. We were drawn to it because of the large expat community there. It's more expensive, but there are more commodities, it's close to the airport, and we feel more connected to the community of people from the US.*
>
> **—Alex V.**

Before Your Deportation

You can't control when your deportation will happen. But you can plan for it. People who have experienced deportation say you should:

- Get an education.
- Learn trades.
- Earn certificates.
- Learn English.

These skills can help you find a job in your new country. This will make your move easier.

☆ For more information on how to create a family plan in case of deportation, see the Prepare for Possible Deportation chapter.

Flori was deported to Guatemala. She said that having a degree and knowing English made it easier to find a job. "If you have some time before you're deported, take advantage of it and go to school," Flori says. "Don't even think about it, just go! There are jobs in Guatemala, but you have to have skills and a diploma. Without that, it's very hard."

The most important thing you can do as a deportee is to make connections while you're still in the States to learn a trade you can do online. That's been a lifesaver for us to be able to secure online work and make US dollars.
—Jennifer V.

If you're in prison and have some time, get your documents in order and your family's. Take any courses you can, any certificates, even if prison-issued, especially anything you can do with your hands: plumbing, carpentry, sheet metal.
—Alex V.

You can also start getting your documents and contacts together. Keep a file that has:

- Your passport
- Phone numbers
- Other important documents
- Your family's documents

Flori says you should give your loved ones' phone number to someone you trust who is detained with you. Ask them to call once your deportation starts. That way your family and friends will know where you are.

While you are in prison or ICE detention, you have the right to get in touch with your country's consulate.

Planning, preparedness can go a long way. Nothing prepares you completely for the shell shock of deportation, but you can make a plan. Create a file with your passport and important documents, phone numbers that are important like your lawyer's and your consulate's.
—Juan Mendez, Honduran Consulate Chicago

The Consulate General of Guatemala
There are 23 Guatemalan consular offices in the US. To find the one nearest you, visit https://minex.gob.gt/Visor_Pagina.aspx?PaginaID=1200 or see our directory in the back of this book.

The Consulate General of Honduras
There are 14 Honduran consular offices in the US. To find the one nearest you, visit https://travel.state.gov/content/travel/en/consularnotification/ConsularNotificationandAccess/Honduras.html or see our directory.

The Consulate General of El Salvador
There are 16 Salvadoran consular offices in the US. To find the one nearest you, visit https://travel.state.gov/content/travel/en/consularnotification/ConsularNotificationandAccess/ElSalvador.html or see our directory.

Your consulate can help you get a temporary ID. This will make it easier for you once you get to your country of origin. They can also help you connect with resources to figure out if you have an asylum case. For a list of organizations that provide legal aid for asylum, see our directory.

Usually, ICE will let family or friends drop a bag for you at the detention center. Call and ask if this is an option. Families can put clothing, toiletries, and even money in the bag. These things will make your deportation much easier.

Deportation takes a long time. It may take months or weeks before you get to your country of origin. Flori was moved to three different places in three months before she went before a judge.

On the day of your deportation, they will probably take your shoelaces and belt. Flori was cuffed at the hands and ankles. She was then moved with men and women going to different countries. You might not get to use a bathroom that day. "Don't drink too much water or coffee," she says. Try to make a friend on the bus or plane, if you can. Having a buddy can make you safer while you're on the move.

> *You're not a criminal. You're not what they say you are.*
>
> **—Alex V.**

Deportation to Guatemala

Deportation is a time of unknowns. You may be worried about who will meet you. Maybe you don't know where you'll end up, or how to create a new life in Guatemala.

This section discusses what happens during deportation. Then it discusses what resources are available once you get there.

☆ For more information on how to create a family plan in case of deportation, see the Make a Plan chapter.

Upon Arrival

You'll arrive in Guatemala by plane at the military airport in Guatemala City (La Aurora Air Force Base). At the airport, you'll get medical care, a snack, and a free phone call. You will also get a chance to exchange money. People from a few organizations will be there to greet you.

People from **CONAMIGUA** will be there. CONAMIGUA stands for Consejo Nacional de Atención al Migrante de Guatemala. They can help you make phone calls to your family to see if they can pick you up. If your family can't get you, they can help you get on the right bus. If you need money, CONAMIGUA can help you get money from other groups or your local government.

CONAMIGUA is a government program. It provides support and help to migrants and their families. CONAMIGUA has offices in Guatemala City, Todos Santos Cuchumatán, Huehuetenango, San Marco, Cobán, Santa Cruz del Quiché, Zacapa, and Petén. Visit their website at conamigua.gob.gt.

The Association of Returned Guatemalans may also meet you at the airport. This group is made up of former US residents. They work to help make the process of moving home easier for people like you. They can help you make local and international phone calls. They can also help you get to the place you're staying. If you don't have a place to stay, they can help you find a shelter or hotel. Visit them on Facebook at https://www.facebook.com/ARG-ong-257316458010435/

The airport is in Guatemala City. Now you'll need to get to your final destination. If you want to stay in the city, the local Episcopalian archdiocese can help. Members of their "Pastoral de Movilidad Humana" are often at the airport. They can help you get to Casa del Migrante. Casa del Migrante provides shelter to returnees. Visit their website at movilidadhumana.com

Be cautious and alert. Armed robberies are common on buses in the city. Gangs and drug traffickers operate throughout the country. Keep your money and valuables secure. Don't use public ATMs. Debit card scams are common.

After Arrival

Fortunately, there are several organizations that help newly arrived people in Guatemala.

Are you staying in Guatemala City? Casa del Migrante can give you shelter for a few days. They also have other services. The organization runs additional facilities in San Marcos and Tecun Uman. Visit their website at casadelmigrantegt.org

Are you moving to the Quetzaltenango area? Colectivo Vida Digna helps migrants and aims to bring back Indigenous culture in the country. Visit their website at vidadignaguatemala.wordpress.com/

For Flori, life in Guatemala was at first scary and exciting. "I was afraid," she says. "Life here is so different. I didn't have nothing. No money, no house, just the clothes I was wearing. But being free was the biggest thing. Being free in my country, I was happy."

Adjusting to this new place will take time. Find family and friends who support you. Have faith in yourself, your abilities, and your strength.

☆ For COVID-19 vaccine information in Guatemala, visit https://www.mspas.gob.gt/covid-19/vacunacion-contra-covid-19/puestos-y-centros-de-vacunacion

Guatemala Resources

Guatemalan Consular Offices in the United States: Assists with getting your ID, ensuring your rights are protected in prison/detention, will help you find contact information for family members, help connect you with resources for health care and education

State/City	Address	Phone/Email	Website
Arizona/ Phoenix	55 E Thomas Rd, 3rd Floor, Suite 300, Phoenix, AZ 85012	(602) 200-3660 consarizona@minex.gob.gt consguatearizona@minex.gob.gt	https://www.minex.gob.gt/
Arizona/ Tucson	100 N Stone Ave #704, Tucson, AZ 85701	(520) 398-7193 constucson@minex.gob.gt	https://www.constucson.minex.gob.gt/?fbclid=IwAROcITfnV0-yeT2kWoDQAo-C_QF7IgfM6ANVPodw7-NFAflYYZhNum2ORLo
California/ San Francisco	659 A Merchant St, San Francisco, CA 94111	(415) 563-8319 conssanfrancisco@minex.gob.gt documentacionsfo@minex.gob.gt	https://www.consulguatesfo.com/ Appointments: https://consulguatesfo.acuityscheduling.com/schedule.php
California/ Los Angelos	1975 Riverside Dr, Los Angelos, CA 90039	(213) 900-1098 conslosangeles@minex.gob.gt	https://minex-gob-gt.my.site.com/pc/s/citas-consulares
California/ San Bernardino	330 N "D" St, Suite #120, San Bernardino, CA 92401	(909) 572-8800 conssanbernardino@minex.gob.gt	https://consulguatesb.acuityscheduling.com/schedule.php
Colorodo/ Denver	1001 S Monaco Pkwy 300, Denver, CO 80224	(303) 629-9212 consdenver@minex.gob.gt jvaley@minex.gob.gt	https://consulguatede.acuityscheduling.com/schedule.php
Florida/ Lake Worth	1926 10th Ave N 104-106, Lake Worth, FL 33461	(561) 660-6223 conslakeworth@minex.gob.gt	https://www.facebook.com/ConsulGuateLakeWorth/
Florida/ Miami	999 Ponce de Leon Blvd 100, 33134	(305) 679-9945 atencionmiami@minex.gob.gt	https://www.facebook.com/ConsGtMiami/

Georgia/ Atlanta	3699 Chamblee Dunwoody Rd, Atlanta, GA, 30341	(470) 657-2510 consatlanta@minex.gob.gt	consatlanta.blogspot.com
Illinois/ Chicago	5559 N Elston Ave #100, Chicago, IL 60630	(312) 540-0781 isanchez@minex.gob.gt	https://consulguatech.acuityscheduling.com/schedule.php
Maryland/ Silver Spring	979 Rollins Avenue Rockville Silver Spring, MD 20852	(240) 485-5050 consmaryland@minex.gob.gt consuladomd@gmail.com	https://app.acuityscheduling.com/schedule.php?owner=11913348
New York/ New York City	276 Park Ave S, Floor 2, New York, NY, 10010	(212) 686-3837 consnewyork@minex.gob.gt	www.consuladoguatemalanuevayork.org www.citaconsularguatemala.com
New York/ Riverhead	1333 E Main St, Suite #1, Riverhead, NY 11901	(631) 405-5010 consriverhead@minex.gob.gt	consriverhead.minex.gob.gt
North Carolina/ Raleigh	6050 Six Forks Rd, Raleigh, NC 27609	(984) 200-1601, (984) 200-2411 consraleigh@minex.gob.gt	consraleigh.minex.gob.gt
Ohio/ Columbus	2105 S Hamilton Rd #100, Columbus, OH 43232	(614) 762-8119	https://app.squarespacescheduling.com/schedule.php?owner=23677258
Oklahoma/ Oklahoma City	5909 NW Expy #100, Oklahoma City, OK 73132	(405) 603-6631, (405) 602-6628 consoklahoma@minex.gob.gt	https://consoklahoma.minex.gob.gt/home/home.aspx
Pennsylvania/ Philadelphia	417 N 8th St, Unit #201, Philadelphia, PA 19123	(267) 322-2044 consphiladelphia@minex.gob.gt hhun@minex.gob.gt	https://www.embassypages.com/guatemala-consulategeneral-philadelphia-unitedstates
Rhode Island/ Providence	555 Valley St, Building 61-321, Providence, RI 02908	(401) 270-6345 consrhodeisland@minex.gob.gt	https://www.facebook.com/ConsGuateRI/
Texas/ Houston	6300 Richmond Ave, Suite 103 Houston, TX 77057	(713) 953-9531 conshouston@minex.gob.gt	https://conshouston.minex.gob.gt/home/Noticia.aspx?id=25912
Texas/ Del Río	106 Foster Dr, Del Río, TX 78840	(830) 422-2230 consdelrio@minex.gob.gt consdelrio@minex.gob.gt	https://www.embassypages.com/guatemala-consulate-delrio-unitedstates
Texas/ Dallas	4405 N Beltwood Pkwy, Farmers Branch, TX 75244	(469) 886-9922 consdallas@minex.gob.gt	https://minex-gob-gt.my.site.com/pc/s/citas-consulares
Texas/ McAllen	705 S Broadway St, McAllen, TX 78501	(956) 429-3412 consmcallen@minex.gob.gt	https://www.facebook.com/ConsulGuateMcAllen/
Washington/ Seattle	18000 International Blvd, S Tower, Suite #1005, Seattle, WA	(206) 693-3600 consseattle@minex.gob.gt cgatica@minex.gob.gt	https://consulguatesea.acuityscheduling.com/schedule.php

Guatemala Resources

Guatemalan Government Institutes

Name	Address	Phone/Email	Website	Description
Guatemala Ministry of Education	6a Calle 1-87 Zona 10, Guatemala	(502) 2411-9595	https://www.mineduc.gob.gt/portal/index.asp	Educational center directory, scholarships, diplomas, educational records
National Council for Attention to Migrants (Conamigua)	5.a avenida "A" 13-28, zona 9, Ciudad Capital	(502) 2299-5600 conamigua@conamigua.gob.gt	https://conamigua.gob.gt/	Migrant assistance
Guatemala Tax Administration (SAT)	Various Locations		https://portal.sat.gob.gt/portal/	Federal tax collection, new business registration
Ministry of Labor and Job Placement	7 Ave 3-33, Zona 9, Edificio Torre Empresarial, Guatemala	(502) 2422-2501	https://www.mintrabajo.gob.gt/	Job fairs, labor protection
Guatemalan Migration Institute	6ta Ave 3-11, Zona 4, Guatemala	(502) 2411-2411	https://igm.gob.gt/	Migrant assistance, passports
National Civil Registry (RENAP)	Calzada Roosevelt 13-46, Zona 7	(502) 2416-1900	https://www.renap.gob.gt/	Birth, marriage, and death certificates
Secretary of Health of Guatemala (MSPAS)	6ta Ave. 3-45, Zona 11, Guatemala	(502) 2444-7474 consultas@mspas.gob.gt	https://www.mspas.gob.gt/	Public hospitals and clinics, COVID-19 vaccine information

Guatemalan Non-Profit Organizations

Name	Address	Phone/Email	Website	Description
Te Conecta	4ta. Avenida 15-70 Zona 10, 3ra Calle 4-44 Zona 10, FLACSO, Guatemala	(502) 2333-6891, (502) 3003-3422 Info@teconectaong.com	https://www.teconecta.org.gt	Information for migrants, job placement
International Organization for Migration (IOM)	3 Avenida 10-35, Zona 9, Guatemala	(502) 2414-7401 iomguatemala@iom.int	https://www.iom.int/countries/guatemala	Psychological support, job training, material support
Desgua	8 Ave. 5-19, Zona 1, Quetzaltenango, Guatemala 09001	DESGUAinfo@desgua.org	https://desgua.org/	Educational and economic support for returned Guatemalans

Guatemalan Non-Profit Organizations

Name	Address	Phone/Email	Website	Description
Guatemalan Association of Returned People		(502) 2294-9217 info@arg.com.gt		Information for deported including transportation help, clothing, emotional support
Guatamala Migrant House	15 Ave. 1-94 "A" Zona 1, Guatemala	(502) 2230-2781 casadelmigrantetecun@gmail.com, migrantetecun@yahoo.com.mx	https://www.scalabriniguate.org/homepage/	Migrant shelter
Brother Pedro's Works	6a Calle Oriente No 20, La Antigua Guatemala	(502) 7931-2100	https://hermanopedrogt.org/	Free health clinic, drug and alcohol addiction services
Norwegian Refugee Council	Ciudad de Guatemala	nrc@nrc.no	https://www.nrc.no/countries/south-america/north-central-america-and-mexico//	Information, counseling and legal assistance to deportees and families
Pop No'j Association	3a Avenida 0-80, Colonia Bran, Zona 3, Ciudad de Guatemala y Kilómetro 287, Naranajales, Colotenango	(502) 2238-0905, (502) 2251-5716 info@asociacionpopnoj.org	https://www.asociacionpopnoj.org/	Guidance, support and resources for migrants
Tecún Umán Migrant House	0 Ave. "C" del Migrante 0-22, Col. Olguita de León, Tecún Umán, San Marcos	(502) 7776-8416 migrantetecun@yahoo.com.mx	https://www.scalabriniguate.org/casa-tecun-uman/	Migrant shelter

Guatemalan Online Resources

Name	Website	Description
Spouses of Deportees Living in Guatemala-Facebook	https://web.facebook.com/groups/DeporteeSpousesLivinginGuatemala	Online support group
The American Friends Service Committee	https://afsc.org/	Detailed online reentry guide

Deportation to Honduras

Maybe you haven't been to Honduras in a long time, or maybe you've lived there recently. No matter what, deportation can be hard and scary. Know that you are not alone. Other people have gone through this before. They can give you advice and encouragement. This section will give you information on deportation to Honduras.

☆ For more information on how to create a family plan in case of deportation, see the Make a Plan chapter.

Upon Arrival

When you are deported, you'll take a plane to the Ramón Villeda Morales airport in San Pedro Sula. You may stop at other places in the US or in Central America first.

You'll be processed at the Centro de Atención al Migrante (CAMR). CAMR says they will give you food and coffee. They can also get you medical care and help you use a phone. They may sometimes give out hygiene kits, too.

You will have to fill out paperwork to prove your identity (constancia). They may also help you get important documents, including a document of "salvoconducto." A salvoconducto lets you travel around the country without any trouble.

This is hopefully what will happen, but some people have not had good experiences. Alex V. was deported in 2014. He says he was offered food. Then, he was told he could make a phone call outside the building. "Then they closed the door on me," he says. "That was all the help I got." Be prepared. You might not get as much help as you need.

According to the official process, you should be interviewed by a volunteer before you leave. If you need help, now is the time to let them know. Sometimes there may be a volunteer from the Red Cross or from the Secretary of State. They can help you find aid. CAMR volunteers can give you a bus voucher to help you get where you need to go. They don't give these to everyone. Let them know you have no money and they will give you a voucher.

You may also be tested for COVID-19 before you leave. If you test positive, you may need to sign a paper promising to stay home for a certain number of days.

It may be the case that you're afraid to return to your home community. If so, the volunteer may refer you to a representative from the Norwegian Refugee Council. The council representative will take you to a private room to get more information. If you are eligible, they will connect you to organizations that can provide protective services.

After your interview, you'll leave for your home. If you live in another part of the country, you'll be taken to Gran Central Metropolitana bus station. Some days, representatives of the Comisión de Acción Social Menonita will be at the station. They can give you a little bit of money.

Be careful. Not everyone gets the help they need from these organizations. Alex V. says that he didn't get any help with transportation. Outside the airport there are taxis waiting. They will charge you a lot of money. Alex V. also says they aren't safe. "Sometimes (the taxis) are used for robbery or kidnapping." If you know anyone nearby, ask them to pick you up or help you with transportation.

Some neighborhoods of San Pedro Sula are very dangerous. Be extra cautious in the city. Do not make eye contact and or speak with people you don't know. Cover any tattoos with long sleeves and pants. Stick close to friends you made on the bus. Do not use a cell phone other than your own to call your family.

> *When I finally got to my hotel, I was exhausted. I had been awake for close to 48 hours. I was traumatized and in shock. I just cried for an hour.*
>
> **—Alex V.**

After Arrival

If you do not have a current ID (cédula in Spanish), get one as soon as possible. Your "cédula" has your national ID number in Honduras. This is like a Social Security number in the US. You will need this for many things. This ID lets you use public clinics and hospitals and buy medicine. It also lets you go to other countries in Central America and bordering states of Mexico for up to nine days.

You can get your ID at your local municipal civil registry. You will need documentation and proof of address. If you don't have those, you can bring two witnesses who can vouch that you are Honduran. Getting an ID can take a while. Deported people say that you should tell the person helping you that it is urgent. You can also offer them a "tip" for their trouble. It may help you get your ID faster.

Sadly, there isn't a lot of support for deportees in Honduras. There are just a few, small programs. The government runs Unidades Municipales de Atención al Retornado (UMAR) in a couple of places. They don't have much to offer, but they can point you to any local organizations that can help.

There is a public hospital in Tegucigalpa called Hospital Escuela. They can help you with medical care and psychiatric evaluations. Catholic churches in your neighborhood may be able to help you with food and clothes.

Tegucigalpa has a Doctors Without Borders clinic. It helps people who have gone through violence, especially sexual violence. They give counseling and STI (sexually transmitted infections) treatment. Doctors Without Borders also runs a mother and child clinic in Choloma. It offers family planning, helps with births, and offers care for victims of sexual violence.

☆ In San Pedro Sula, there is a growing call center industry. They need employees who have English speaking skills and knowledge of computers.

Honduras Resources

Honduran Consular Offices in the United States: Assists with getting your ID, ensuring your rights are protected in prison/detention, will help you find contact information for family members, help connect you with resources for health care and education

State/City	Address	Phone/Email	Website
Arizona/ Phoenix	4040 E McDowell Rd #305, Phoenix, AZ 85008	(602) 273-0173	
California/ Los Angeles	3550 Wilshire Blvd, Unit #320, Los Angeles, CA 90010	(818) 739-2121 infoconsuladola@gmail.com	https://www.embassypages.com/honduras-consulategeneral-losangeles-unitedstates
Florida/ Miami	777 NW 72nd Avenue.12-Jan-2023	(305) 269-3930 info@consuladohn.com	https://embassies.info/ConsulateofHondurasinMiamiFlorida
Georgia/ Atlanta	6755 Peachtree Industrial Blvd, Ste 120 Atlanta, GA 30360 United States	(770) 645-8881 info@consuladohnatl.com	http://www.consuladohnatl.com

Deportation to Central America

Illinois/ Chicago	6200 N Hiawatha Ave Penthouse, Chicago, IL 60646	(470) 751-9077 consulchicago@gmail.com	https://www.facebook.com/pages/Consulado-de-Honduras-en-Chicago/543407172443161
Louisiana/ New Orleans	1250 Poydras St Suite #100, New Orleans, LA 70113, United States	(504) 228-3348 info@nolahn.com	citaconsular.sreci.gob.hn
New York/ New York City	120 W 23rd Street New York, NY 10011 United States	(212) 714-9451 info.consuladodehonduras.ny@gmail.com	https://embassies.info/ConsulateofHondurasinNewYork
Texas/ Dallas	2520 W Irving Blvd #400, Irving TX 75061	(972) 986-5110 info.consuladodehonduras.ny@gmail.com	https://www.embassypages.com/honduras-consulate-dallas-unitedstates
Texas/ McAllen	1209 Galveston Ave McAllen, TX 78501	(470) 751-9077 consuladohnmcallen@outlook.es	https://www.facebook.com/people/Consulado-de-Honduras-en-McAllen-Texas/100064322366806/
Texas/ Houston	3731 Briarpark Dr #155, Houston, TX 77042	(346) 201-6711 consuladohonduras houston@gmail.com	https://www.embassypages.com/honduras-consulategeneral-houston-unitedstates
Washington/ Seattle	1107 Grady Way, Suite #100, Renton, WA 98057	(206) 420-0947 proteccionconsularseattle@gmail.com	http://citaconsular.sreci.gob.hn/citaconsular/pages/layout/CitaConsular.php
Washington DC/ Washington DC	1528 K Street, N. W. Floor 2 Washington D.C., DC 20006	(202) 773-2972, (202) 773-2978 onsul.hondurasdcusa@verizon.net	https://www.embassypages.com/honduras-embassy-washingtondc-unitedstates

Honduran Government Institutes

Name	Address	Phone/Email	Website	Description
Honduras Tax Administration	Edificio Cuerpo Bajo "A" Bulevar Juan Pablo II, Centro Cívico Gubernamental José Cecilio del Valle, Tegucigalpa	(504) 2216-5800 asistencia@sar.gob.hn	https://www.sar.gob.hn/	Tax administration

Honduran Government Institutes

Name	Address	Phone/Email	Website	Description
Returned Migrant Attention Center (CAMR)	Juan Ramón Molina, Antiguo Edificio del Banco Central, Tegucigalpa	(504) 2236-0200 asesoriacamr@hotmail.com, alhovoz@sre.gob.hn, alhovozhonduras@gmail.com	https://conmigho.hn/centro-de-atencion-al-migrante-retornado-omoa/	Attention upon arrival, meal, transportation help, medical and psychological attention
Secretary of Labor and Social Security	Cuerpo Bajo B, Centro Cívico Gubernamental José Cecilio del Valle, Boulevard Juan Pablo II., Tegucigalpa	(504) 2242-7830	http://www.trabajo.gob.hn/	Job fairs, labor protection
Secretary of Public Health (SEDESA)	Barrio El Centro, Avenida Cervantes, Calle El Telegrafo, Contiguo Avenida Miguel Cervantes, Tecgucigalpa	(504) 2222-5771	www.salud.gob.hn/	Health services, attention to gender violence
National Registry of Persons	Col Palmira, frente a Distrito Hotelero Plaza San Martín, Tegucigalpa	respuesta@rnp.hn	https://rnlpm61prd-aucrnph01.cec.ocp.oraclecloud.com/site/HOME/	Birth certificates and identification
Secretary of Education	Primera Avenida entre Segunda y Tercera calle, Comayagüela	(504) 2226-6200	https://www.se.gob.hn/	Virtual education center, diplomas, educational records

Honduran Non-Profit Organizations

Name	Address	Phone/Email	Website	Description
Red Cross	Ave 2, Barrio Concepción, Tegucigalpa	(504) 2237-1800	https://www.icrc.org/en/where-we-work/americas/honduras	Migrant services including medical care, water, phone call to family
Norwegian Refugee Council	Various Locations	nrc@nrc.no	https://www.nrc.no/countries/south-america/north-central-america-and-mexico//	Information, counseling and legal assistance to deportees and families
International Organization for Migration (IOM)	Col Palmira, 3ra avenida, Calle del Brasil, Bloque 3, Casa 12	(504) 2237-7460 iomtegucigalpa@iom.int	https://www.iom.int/countries/honduras	Psychological support, job training, material support

Honduran Non-Profit Organizations

Name	Address	Phone/Email	Website	Description
Casa Alianza	Calle Morelos, Avenida Cervantes, Frente Optica Matamoros, Tegucialpa	(504) 2237-3623 contacto@casa-alianza.org.hn	http://casa-alianza.org.hn/new.casa-alianza.org.hn/?fbclid=IwAR34CAw8coipVnrJM9Jwk8t0BanyW0ExGCYMo2Edftcb3-C1P0sewlwD7I	Child/youth migrant shelter
Mennonite Social Action Commission (CASM)	Barrio Guadalupe, 21 y 22 Calle, 3. Ave. N.E. Casa 2114, San Pedro Sula, Cortés	(504) 2553-5437 casm@casm.hn	https://casm.hn	Agricultural, health and education programs thoroughout the country
National Forum for Migration in Honduras	Col Palmira, Calzada Los Olivos, Casa No. 352, a un costado del Edificio Italia, Tegucigalpa	(504) 2205-8396 fonamih@yahoo.com	www.fonamihn.org/	Association of organizations that work with migrants, Human rights defense
Ocotepeque Migrant House	Basílica Nuestra Señora de Suyapa	(504) 2557-1651 liflores@unicah.edu		Migrant shelter

Honduran Online Resources

Name	Website	Description
The American Friends Service Committee	https://afsc.org/	Detailed online reentry guide

Deportation to El Salvador

Returning to a country after deportation can be scary. You may feel worried or lonely. You may feel anxious about going to a new place where you don't know anyone. Maybe you will be with your family again, but you haven't seen them for years. Know that you are not alone. There are organizations and resources available to help you in your journey. This section will give you information on deportation to El Salvador.

☆ For more information on how to create a family plan in case of deportation, see the Make a Plan chapter.

Upon Arrival

Flights take off Monday through Friday from the US to the Oscar Arnulfo Romero International Airport. When you get there, people from the Directorate of Assistance to Migrants (DAMI) will meet you. They will take you by bus to the DAMI headquarters in San Salvador.

A word of caution: the DAMI headquarters is next to the a known gang territory. If you don't know the area, ask DAMI for help with transport and directions. Coyotes and scammers are often around DAMI. They may offer you a ride or a stay at a hotel. Do not accept these offers or give them money.

At the DAMI offices, you'll wait in the reception room. Someone from DAMI will explain the steps you'll follow to help you get where you need to go. If you live outside San Salvador, you'll go first. People who live in San Salvador will go next.

These steps aren't necessarily in order. Everyone goes through them in a different order based on their situation.

1. The first step is a short interview with the General Directorate of Migration and Aliens. They'll ask for basic information like:
    - Your name, age, and gender
    - Why you moved to the US
    - How long you were in the US
    - Where you lived and worked
    - If you still have family in the US
    - If you were abused during the deportation process
    - Contact information in El Salvador, if you have it

   If your belongings were held during deportation, you can ask for them now.

2. The National Civil Police does the second step. If you have any criminal charges in El Salvador, the police will process you now. Did you leave El Salvador because of violence, like human trafficking? You can file a complaint about it now.

3. Next, you'll get medical care from the Ministry of Health. They will offer you a checkup and a psychological diagnosis. They can also refer you to a health center near your home. You can refuse this service if you choose.

4. Next, you'll speak with the Ministry of Foreign Affairs. They can help you contact your family members both inside and outside El Salvador. You can also ask about claiming property and signing up for benefits through social programs.

5. The fifth step is for women who have gone through violence in El Salvador or other countries. This step is run by the Salvadoran Institute for the Development of Women. They can get you legal help.

6. Have you lost your Unique Identity Document? The National Registry of Natural Persons can help you get a new one.

While at DAMI, you can also use the phone and internet. They will give you clothes if you need them. Do you plan to leave the city? The General Directorate of Migration and Aliens can help you with bus fare.

When you finish the steps at NAMI, you'll go to the waiting room. If your friends or family are picking you up, they will be waiting there. If not, a DAMI bus will take you to the main bus station in San Salvador. You can get a bus to your final destination there.

If you need a place to stay, the Migrant Assistance Center can give you shelter. You'll need to prove that you have no one to stay with in San Salvador. You'll also need to prove you don't have the money to pay for a hotel. You can also show them that there is no bus to your city or town.

After Arrival

Sadly, there are not a lot of programs to help returned migrants in El Salvador. See the directory on the next page for a few.

The Ministry of Foreign Affairs and the Ministry of Labor can help you with technical training, training on how to apply for jobs, and some seed money. They also have a tool to help you find job openings. You can visit the Ministry of Foreign Affairs online at www.rree.gob.sv and the Ministry of Labor at www.mtps.gob.sv.

El Salvador Resources

Salvadoran Consular Offices in the United States: Assists with getting your ID, ensuring your rights are protected in prison/detention, will help you find contact information for family members, help connect you with resources for health care and education

State/City	Address	Phone/Email	Website
Arizona/ Tucson	1039 N 6th Ave, Tucson, AZ 85705	(888) 301-1130 consuladotucson@rree.gob.sv	https://www.facebook.com/ConsulTucsonSV/
California/ Los Angeles	3450 Wilshire Blvd #550, Los Angeles, CA 90010	(213) 234-9200 consuladoesla@rree.gob.sv	https://locator.lacounty.gov/lac/Location/3176563/consulate-general-of-el-salvador
California/ San Francisco	507 Polk St #280, San Francisco, CA 94102	(415) 771-8524, (888) 301-1130 consuladosanfrancisco@rree.gob.sv	
California/ San Diego	353 Church Ave A, Chula Vista, CA 91910	(619) 585-8883 esconsulsd@sbcglobal.net	
California/ Oakland	International Blvd 2B, Oakland, CA 94603	(510) 635-1700 infoEEUU@rree.gob.sv	
Colorodo/ Denver	1450 S Havana St #100, Aurora, CO 80012	(888) 301-1130 consuladoaurora@rree.gob.sv	https://www.facebook.com/ConsulAuroraSV/
Florida/ Miami	8550 NW 33rd St #100, Doral, FL 33122	(305) 799-2530 consuladosv-doralfl@rree.gob.sv	https://www.facebook.com/ConsulDoralSV/

Georgia/ Atlanta	3550 Corporate Way A, 30096	(888) 301-1130 consuladoatlanta@rree.gob.sv	https://www.embassypages.com/elsalvador-consulategeneral-atlanta-unitedstates
Illinois/ Chicago	177 N State Mezzanine, Chicago, IL 60601	(312) 332-1393, (312) 578-5390 consuladochicago@rree.gob.sv	www.facebook.com/CGES21
Maryland/ Silver Spring	926 Philadelphia Ave, Silver Spring, MD 20910	(240) 670-7509 consuladoelsalvadordc@gmail.com, consuladoespasaportedc@gmail.com	www.facebook.com/consuladoelsalvadorsilverspring/
Massachusetts/ Boston	46 Bennington E St, Boston, MA 02128	(617) 567-8338, (617) 567-8484 consuladoboston@rree.gob.sv, consuladoboston@gmail.com	www.facebook.com/Consulado-General-de-El-Salvador-Boston-Massachusetts-409513465810925/
Nevada/ Las Vegas	765 N Nellis Blvd C-5, Las Vegas, NV 89110	(702) 437-5337, (702) 437-5339 consuladolasvegas2@gmail.com, consuladolasvegas@rree.gob.sv	www.facebook.com/ConsuladoLV
New Jersey/ Newark	40 Parker Rd #100, Elizabeth, NJ 07208	(908) 820 0881 consuladonewjersey@rree.gob.sv	https://www.embassypages.com/elsalvador-consulate-newark-unitedstates
New York/ New York	12 W 37th St, New York, NY 10018	(212) 889-3608 consuladonyc@rree.gob.sv	www.facebook.com/consuladonyc/
New York/ Brentwood	151 Alkier St, Brentwood, Long Island, NY 11717	(888) 301-1130 comunicacioneslongisland@gmail.com, consuladobrentwood@gmail.com, consuladolongisland@rree.gob.sv	https://www.embassypages.com/elsalvador-consulategeneral-brentwood-unitedstates
North Carolina/ Charlotte	1520 W Blvd C, Charlotte, NC 28208	(888) 301-1130 consuladocharlotte@rree.gob.sv	www.facebook.com/ConsulCharlotteSV/
Texas/ Houston	8300 Bissonet St #400, Houston, TX 77074	(888) 301-1130 tramiteshouston@rree.gob.sv	www.facebook.com/CGESHoustonSV
Texas/ Dallas	7610 N Stemmons Fwy, Suite 400, Dallas, TX 75235	(888) 301-1130 portalcitas.rree.gob.sv	https://www.facebook.com/ConsulDallasSV/
Texas/ Laredo	6010 McPherson Rd #140, Laredo, TX 78041	(888) 301-1130 consuladosv-laredotx@rree.gob.sv	https://www.facebook.com/ConsulLaredoSV/

Texas/ McAllen	701 S Broadway St, McAllen, TX 78501	(888) 301-1130 consuladomcallen@rree.gob.sv	https://www.facebook.com/ConsulMcAllenSV/
Texas/ El Paso	400 W San Antonio B, El Paso, TX	(888) 301-1130 consuladoelpasotx@rree.gob.sv	www.facebook.com/ConsuladoSVELP/
Utah/ Salt Lake City	124 S 400 E #410, Salt Lake City, UT 84111	(888) 301-1130 consuladosaltlakecity@rree.gob.sv	https://www.consulate-info.com/consulate/22129/El-Salvador-in-Salt-Lake-City
Virginia/ Woodbridge	14572 Potomac Mills Rd #12, Woodbridge, VA 22192	(703) 490-4300 consuladosaltlakecity@rree.gob.sv	https://www.facebook.com/ConWoodbridgeSV/
Washington Seattle	615 2nd Ave #50, Seattle, WA 98104	(206) 971 7950 consuladoseattle@rree.gob.sv	www.facebook.com/consuladoESSeattle

Salvadoran Government Institutes

Name	Address	Phone/Email	Website	Description
Health Ministry	Calle Arce #827, San Salvador	(503) 2591-7000 webmaster@salud.gob.sv	www.salud.gob.sv/	Health services, COVID-19 information
Education Ministry	Alamada Juan Pablo II y Calle Guadalupe , Edificio A, San Salvador	(503) 2592-2000 educacion@mined.gob.sv	https://www.mined.gob.sv/	Educational center directory, diplomas, educational records
Labor Ministry	Alameda Juan Pablo II y 17 Ave Nte Edificios 2, 3 y 4, Centro de Gobierno, San Salvador	(503) 2529-3700 buzon.sugerencias@mtps.gob.sv	https://www.mtps.gob.sv/	Job fairs and announcements
Migrant Attention and Protection Office	9 Poniente y 15 Av N, San Salvador	(503) 2213-7700 usuarios@seguridad.gob.sv	www.migracion.gob.sv/	Reception of returning Salvadorans
Foreign Relations Ministry	Blvd Cancillería , Calle El Pedregal, Antiguo Cuscatlan, La Libertad	(503) 2555-8500	https://sansalvador.ilea.state.gov/contact	Passports, visa, information about reuniting family abroad in El Salvador
National Registry	Alameda Manuel Enrique Araujo, Edificio Carbonell N° 1, Colonia Roma, San Salvador	(503) 2521-9300 info@rnpn.gob.sv	https://www.rnpn.gob.sv/	Birth certificates, idenitification
National Council for the Protection and Development of Migrants (CONMIGRANTES)		conmigrantes@rree.gob.sv	https://www.latinno.net/en/case/9065/	Human rights protection, national development, job postings

Salvadoran Non-Profit Organizations

Name	Address	Phone/Email	Website	Description
U.S. Committee for Refugees and Immigrants (USCRI)	Col San Francisco, Calle Los Bambués y Calle Los Abetos, 37-A y B, San Salvador	(503) 2526-9219 eolan@uscrica.org	http://refugees.org/field-office/central-america/	Connection to resources to meet basic needs, legal representation
Cáritas of El Salvador	Av Olímpica y Pasaje 3, Casa #130, San Salvador	(503) 2511-4300 info@caritas.sv	http://www.caritas.sv/	Social services, economic development
Red Cross	Calle 2, Santa Lucía, San Salvador	(503) 2294-0969, (503) 2239-4942	https://cruzrojasal.org.sv/	Zika, dengue and chikungunya prevention
Scalabrini Migrant House	Col Mugdan 6ta, Ave N, Passage Viaud 716 503, San Salvador	(503) 2221-9725 migrantesv@gmail.com	https://www.migrantes.com.mx/san-salvador	Migrant shelter
Committee of Families of Disappeared and Deceased Migrants of El Salvador (COFAMIDE)	Centro Histórico, San Salvador	(503) 7602-2625 cofamide.elsalvador@yahoo.com, contact@martinbarofund.org	http://martinbarofund.org/cofamide-2017/	Psychological support and advocacy
International Organization for Migration (IOM)	Urbanización Madre Selva, Pasaje H # 5 01101 Antiguo Cuscatlán, El Salvador	(503) 2521-0500 cofamide.elsalvador@yahoo.com, contact@martinbarofund.org	https://triangulonorteca.iom.int/es/el-salvador	Migrant worker protection
Norwegian Refugee Council	San Salvador	nrc@nrc.no	https://www.nrc.no/countries/south-america/north-central-america-and-mexico//	Information, counseling and legal assistance to deportees and families
Alliance of Returned Salvadorans (ALSARE)	Boulevard Los Héroes, Condominio Los Héroes, Séptimo Nivel, Apartamento No. 7-D 503, San Salvador	(202) 360-4530 alsat.retornados16@gmail.com	https://www.iaf.gov/es/grants/el-salvador/2018-alsare/	Connection to resources to meet basic needs, psychological assistance

Salvadoran Online Resources

Name	Website	Description
The American Friends Service Committee	https://afsc.org/	Detailed online reentry guide

Part 5: Directory

- Immigration Resources in the US
    - Legal Aid and Immigration Services
    - Mexican Consular Offices
    - Secretary of State Offices for Apostille Services
- Mexico Resources
    - Mexico National Resources
    - Mexico City Resources
    - Matamoros, Tamaulipas
    - Reynosa, Tamaulipas
    - Ciudad Juárez, Chihuahua
    - Tijuana, Baja California
    - Nogales, Sonora
    - Hermosillo, Sonora
    - Cancún, Quintana Roo
    - San Miguel de Allende, Guanajuato
    - Leon, Guanajuato
    - Cabo San Lucas, Baja California Sur
    - Puebla, Puebla
    - Guadalajara, Jalisco
    - Monterrey, Nuevo León
    - Ecatepec, Estado de México

Immigration Resources in the US

United States National Resources: Immigrant advocacy orgs, legal aid that works with immigrants, national or regional, or state or local, (primarily from Mexico, Honduras, Guatemala, El Salvador)

Name	Address	Phone/Email	Website	Description
ACLU (American Civil Liberties Union)	125 Broad Street, 18th Floor New York, NY 10004	(212) 549-2500	https://www.aclu.org/issues/immigrants-rights?redirect=immigrants-rights	Protects the rights of immigrants in our communities
Al Otro Lado	511 E San Ysidro Blvd #333 San Ysidro, CA 92173	(664) 208-8994 info@alotrolado.org	https://alotrolado.org/	Holistic legal and humanitariansupport to refugees, deportees, andother migrants in the US and Tijuana
American Bar Assocation Commission on Immigration	ABA Commission on Immigration 1050 Connecticut Ave NW #400 Washington, DC 20036	(800) 285-2221 immcenter@americanbar.org	https://www.americanbar.org/groups/public_interest/immigration/	Education and policy, pro bono legal services for asylum seekers in South Texas and San Diego, training for those working with children in immigration
American Friends Service Committee	1501 Cherry St, Philadelphia, PA 19102	(215) 241-7000	https://www.afsc.org/xs	Provides the guide Crossing South, resources for people returning to México, Honduras, El Salvador, and Guatemala
American Immigration Council	1331 G St NW, Suite #200, Washington DC 20005	(202) 507-7500 info@immcouncil.org	https://www.americanimmigrationcouncil.org	Immigration education, training and tools for attorneys, cultural exchange program, fellowship opportunities, policy, and advocacy work
American Immigration Lawyers Association	1331 G St NW, Suite #300, Washington DC 20005	(202) 507-7600 membership@aila.org	https://www.aila.org/	National association of attorneys and law professors who practice and teach immigration law. Members provide legal services
ASISTA	PO Box 12 Suffield, CT 06078	(860) 758-0733 questions@asistahelp.org	https://asistahelp.org	Provides training for those providing legal services to immigrant survivors of crime, advocacy work, and skill training for immigrant survivors

Immigration Resources in the US

BorderAngels	2258 Island Ave, San Diego, CA 92102	(619) 487-0249 admin@borderangels.org	https://www.borderangels.org	Advocacy and services, including education, water drops, bond fund program, and shelter aid
CAIR (Capital Area Immigrants' Rights Coalition) Washington DC	1025 Connecticut Ave NW #701, Washington DC 20036		https://www.caircoalition.org	Legal representation for detained immigrant children and adults
Catholic Charities	2050 Ballenger Ave, Suite #400, Alexandria, VA 22314	(703) 549-1390 info@catholiccharitiesusa.org	https://www.catholiccharitiesusa.org/our-vision-and-ministry/immigration-refugee-services/	Citizenship education, community outreach and education, immigration and legal services
CLINIC (Catholic Legal Immigration Network)	8757 Georgia Avenue, Suite 850, Silver Spring, MD 20910	(301) 565-4800 national@cliniclegal.org	https://cliniclegal.org/	Legal services directory, religious immigration services, and advocates for the rights of immigrants
Free Them All		freethemallva@protonmail.com	https://medium.com/free-them-all-va	Supports those incarcerated in Virginia detention centers, jails, and prisons
Freedom for Immigrants	1322 Webster St Suite 300, Oakland, CA 94612, United States	(510) 822-2722 rmerton@freedomforimmigrants.org	https://www.freedomforimmigrants.org	Advocates for the rights of immigrants, runs a national detention and abuse reporting hotline
HIAS (Hebrew Immigrant Aid Society)	1300 Spring St #500, Silver Spring, MD 20910	(212) 967-4100, Toll-free: 800-HIAS-714 info@hias.org	https://www.hias.org/	Refugee resettlement, legal services for immigrants, advocacy
Immigrant Defenders Law Center	634 S Spring St, 10th Fl, Los Angeles, CA 90014	(213) 634-0999 info@immdef.org	https://www.immdef.org/	Legal immigration services
Immigrant Families Together			https://immigrantfamiliestogether.com	Support for families separated at the border, assistance for those in detention, humanitarian aid
Immigrant Legal Resouces Center			https://www.ilrc.org/	Education and leadership development for immigrant communities, advocacy

Immigration Resources in the US

Immigration Advocates Network			https://www.immigrationadvocates.org/	Access to immigration legal resources and information
Immigration Justice Campaign	1331 G St NW, Suite #200, Washington, DC 20005	campaignwebsite@immcouncil.org	https://immigrationjustice.us/	Legal services and advocacy
Interfaith Community for Detained Immigrants	303 East Wacker Drive, Suite 2108 Chicago, IL 60601	(708) 297-4065 hello@icdichicago.org	https://www.icdichicago.org	Transit and housing assistance, wrap-around services for asylum seekers, advocacy
Just Neighbors Ministry	7630 Little River Turnpike #900, Annandale, VA 22003, United States	(703) 979-1240 info@justneighbors.org	https://www.justneighbors.org/	Legal immigration services
La Posada Providencia	30094 Marydale Rd, San Benito, TX 78586	(956) 399-3826 cdplaposada@lppshelter.org	https://lppshelter.org	24/7 Emergency shelter (food, shower, laundry, internet, clothes, transportation, English classes, employment services, paperwork help)
Lutheran Immigration and Refugee Services	700 Light Street, Baltimore, Maryland 21230	(410) 983-4000	https://www.lirs.org/	Refugee resettlement and family reunification services, new American services
National Immigrant Justice Center	224 S. Michigan Ave., Suite 600, Chicago, IL 60604	312-660-1370 immigrantlegaldefense@heartlandalliance.org	https://immigrantjustice.org	General immigration services, asylum, detained immigrants, human trafficking, LGBTQ immigrant, immigration court help desk, services for unaccompanied immigrant children
National Immigration Law Center Headquarters	3450 Wilshire Blvd. #108 – 62 Los Angeles, CA 90010	(213) 639-3900 reply@nilc.org	https://www.nilc.org	Advocates for immigrants with low income
National Immigration Project of the National Lawyers Guild	2201 Wisconsin Ave NW #200, Washington, DC 20007	(617) 227-9727	https://nipnlg.org	Criminal and deportation defense, advocacy for victims of crimes, legal support and advocacy

Immigration Resources in the US

National Network for Immigrant and Refugee Rights	310 8th St #310, Oakland, CA 94607	(510) 465-1984 nnirr@nnirr.org	https://nnirr.org	Advocates for immigrants and refugees
probono.net	151 W 30th St, 6th Floor, New York, NY 10001		https://www.probono.net/	Connections to legal services and legal information
RAICES (The Refugee and Immigrant Center For Education and Legal Services)	1305 N Flores St, San Antonio, TX 78212		https://www.raicestexas.org/what-we-do/	Legal services for immigrants with low-income
Team Brownsville		info@teambrownsville.org	https://www.teambrownsville.org	Food, shelter, water for asylum seekers in Matamoros, Reynosa, Brownville Bus Station
The Immigration Project	PO Box 1503, Bloomington, IL 61702	(309) 829-8703 infoimmigration project.org	https://www.immigrationproject.org/	Immigration-related legal and educational services
UnidosUS	1126 16th St NW #600, Washington DC 20036	(202) 785-1670	https://www.unidosus.org	Latino civil rights and advocacy organization. Hosts an affiliate network of 300 community-based organizations in US

United States Secretary of State Offices: Apostille services of original notarized documents with official signature for a fee of $5. Include name of country where document will be used and a self-addressed stamped envelope.

State/City	Name	Address	Phone/Email	Website
Alabama/ Montgomery	**Alabama Secretary of State**	P.O. Box 5616 Montgomery, Alabama 36103-5616	(334) 242-7200 Wes.Allen@sos.alabama.gov	https://www.sos.alabama.gov/administrative-services/authentications
Alaska/ Juneau	**Alaska Lt. Governor**	PO Box 110015, Juneau, AK 99811	(907) 465-3509 April Simpson – apostille@alaska.gov	https://ltgov.alaska.gov/notaries-public/authentications-and-apostilles/
Arizona/ Tuscon	**Arizona Secretary of State**	400 W Congress #141, Tuscon, AZ 85701	(602) 542-6187	https://azsos.gov/services/document-authentication-apostille

Immigration Resources in the US

Arizona/ Phoenix	Arizona Secretary of State	1700 W Washington St, Fl 7, Phoenix, AZ 85007	(602) 542-6187	https://azsos.gov/services/document-authentication-apostille
Arkansas/ Little Rock	Arkansas Secretary of State	500 Woodlane Ave #256, Little Rock, AR 72201	(501) 682-1010 capitolevents@sos.arkansas.gov	https://www.sos.arkansas.gov/business-commercial-services-bcs/for-apostille-certification
California/ Sacramento	California Secretary of State	1500 11th St, Sacramento, CA 95814	(916) 653-6814	https://www.sos.ca.gov/
California/ Los Angeles	California Secretary of State	300 S Spring St #12513, Los Angeles, CA 90013	(213) 897-3062	https://www.sos.ca.gov/notary/request-apostille
Colorado/ Denver	Colorado Secretary of State	1700 Broadway, Suite #550, Denver, CO 80290	(303) 894-2200	https://www.sos.state.co.us/pubs/apostilles/general.html www.coloradosos.gov
Connecticut/ Hartford	Connecticut Secretary of State	165 Capitol Ave, Suite #1000, Hartford, CT 06106	(860) 509-6200	https://portal.ct.gov/SOTS/Legislative-Services/Authenticationof-Documents-and-the-Apostille
Delaware/ Dover	Delaware Secretary of State	401 Federal St, #4, Dover, DE 19901	(302) 739-3073 corp@delaware.gov	https://corp.delaware.gov/
Florida/ Tallahassee	Florida Department of State	2415 N Monroe St, Suite #810, Tallahassee, FL 32303	(850) 245-6000 CorpHelp@dos.myflorida.com	https://dos.myflorida.com/sunbiz/
Georgia/ Atlanta	Georgia Superior Court Clerks' Cooperative Authority	1875 Century Blvd, Suite #100, Atlanta, GA 30345	(404) 327-9060 Help@gsccca.org	https://www.gsccca.org/
Hawaii/ Honululu	Hawaii Lt. Governor	Hawaii State Capitol, 415 S Beretania St., Floor 5, Honolulu, HI 96813	(808) 586-0255	https://ltgov.hawaii.gov/

Idaho/ Boise	Idaho Secretary of State	700 W. Jefferson St, Room E205 Boise, ID 83702	(208) 334-2852 govsvc@sos.idaho.gov	https://sos.idaho.gov
Illinois/ Springfield	Illinois Secretary of State	111 E Monroe St, Springfield, IL 62756	(800) 252-8980 islinfo@ilsos.gov	https://www.ilsos.gov/
Illinois/ Chicago	Illinois Secretary of State	17 N State St #1010, Chicago, IL 60602	(800) 252-8980 islinfo@ilsos.gov	https://www.ilsos.gov/
Indiana/ Indianapolis	Indiana Secretary of State	302 W Washington St #E018, Indianapolis, IN 46204	(800) 457-8283	https://www.in.gov/sos/
Iowa/ Des Moines	Iowa Secretary of State	321 E 12th St, 1st Floor, Des Moines, IA 50319	(888) 767-8683 sos@sos.iowa.gov	https://sos.iowa.gov/business/FormsAndFees.html
Kansas/ Topeka	Kansas Secretary of State	120 SW 10th, First Floor, Topeka, KS 66612	(785) 296-4564 kssos@ks.gov	https://sos.ks.gov/index.html
Kentucky/ Frankfort	Kentucky Secretary of State	700 Capital Ave #152 Frankfort, KY 40601	(502) 564-3490	https://www.sos.ky.gov/Pages/default.aspx
Louisiana/ Baton Rouge	Louisiana Secretary of State	8585 Archives Ave, Baton Rouge, LA 70809	(225) 922-2880	https://www.sos.la.gov/NotaryAndCertifications/Certifications/AuthenticateSignaturesOfLouisianaOfficials/Pages/default.aspx
Maine/ Augusta	Maine Secretary of State	101 State House Station, Augusta, ME 04333	(207) 624-7736	https://www.maine.gov/sos/cec/apostilles/
Maryland/ Annapolis	Maryland Secretary of State	16 Francis St, Annapolis, MD 21401	(410) 974-5521	https://sos.maryland.gov/Certifications/Pages/default.aspx
Massachusetts/ Springfield	Massachusetts Secretary of the Commonwealth	436 Dwight St #102, Springfield, MA 01103	(800) 392-6090 cis@sec.state.ma.us	https://www.sec.state.ma.us/
Massachusetts/ Fall River	Massachusetts Secretary of the Commonwealth	218 S Main St #206, Fall River, MA 02721	(800) 392-6090 cis@sec.state.ma.us	https://www.sec.state.ma.us/

Immigration Resources in the US

Michigan/ Lansing	**Michigan Secretary of State**	7064 Crowner Dr, Lansing, MI 48918	(888) 767-6424	https://www.michigan.gov/sos
Minnesota/ Saint Paul	**Minnesota Secretary of State**	332 Minnesota St, Suite #N201, Saint Paul, MN 55101	(651) 296-2803, (877) 551-6767	https://www.sos.state.mn.us/
Mississippi/ Jackson	**Mississippi Secretary of State**	125 S Congress St, Jackson, MS 39201	(601) 359-1633 secretary@sos.ms.gov	https://sos.ms.gov/business-services/apostilles-authentications
Missouri/ Jefferson City	**Missouri Secretary of State**	600 W Main #322, Jefferson City, MO 65101	(573) 751-2783 Info@sos.mo.gov	https://s1.sos.mo.gov/business/notary/notary/certify
Montana/ Helena	**Montana Secretary of State**	Montana Capitol Building, Rm 260, Helena, MT 59620-2801	(406) 444-2034	https://sosmt.gov/
Nebraska/ Lincoln	**Nebraska Secretary of State**	1445 K Street, #2300 Lincoln, NE 68508	(402) 471-2554	https://sos.nebraska.gov/
Nevada/ Carson City	**Nevada Secretary of State**	101 N Carson Street Suite 3 Carson City, NV 89701	(775) 684-5708 sosmail@sos.nv.gov	https://www.nvsos.gov/sos/businesses/apostille
New Hampshire/ Concord	**New Hampshire Secretary of State**	107 N Main St #204, Concord, NH 03301	(603) 271-3242 elections@sos.nh.gov	https://www.sos.nh.gov/
New Jersey/ Trenton	**New Jersey Treasury**	PO Box 452 Trenton, NJ 08646	(609) 292-9292	https://www.state.nj.us/treasury/revenue/apostilles.shtml
New Mexico/ Santa Fe	**New Mexico Secretary of State**	325 Don Gaspar #300, Santa Fe, NM 87501	(505) 827-3600, (800) 477-3632 Business.Services@state.nm.us	https://www.sos.nm.gov/
New York/ Albany	**New York Department of State**	PO Box 22001, Albany, NY 12201	(518) 474-4429 licensing@dos.ny.gov	https://dos.ny.gov/apostille-or-certificate-authentication

Immigration Resources in the US

North Carolina/ Raleigh	**North Carolina Secretary of State**	PO Box 29622, Raleigh, NC 27626	(919) 814-5400	https://www.sosnc.gov/divisions/authentications/apostille_certificates
North Dakota/ Bismark	**North Dakota Secretary of State**	600 E Blvd Ave, Dept 108, Bismarck, ND 58505	(701) 328-2900, (800) 352-0867	https://sos.nd.gov/notaries-public/authentications-apostille-and-certification.html
Ohio/ Columbus	**Ohio Secretary of State**	22 N 4th St, Columbus, OH 43215	(614) 728-9200, (877) 767-3453	https://www.ohiosos.gov/records/apostilles-certifications/
Oklahoma/ Oklahoma City	**Oklahoma Secretary of State**	421 NW 13th St #210, Oklahoma City, OK 73103	(405) 521-4211	https://www.sos.ok.gov/business/apostilles.aspx
Oregon/ Salem	**Oregon Secretary of State**	255 Capitol St NE #151, Salem, OR 97310	(503) 986-2200	https://sos.oregon.gov/business/pages/how-to-get-authentication-apostille.aspx
Pennsylvania/ Harrisburg	**Pennsylvania Secretary of State**	Bureau of Commissions, Elections and Legislation, Room 210 N Office Building, Harrisburg, PA 17120	(717) 787-5280	https://www.dos.pa.gov/OtherServices/Certifications_Apostilles/Pages/How-Do-I-Obtain-an-Apostille-or-Certification.aspx
Rhode Island/ Providence	**Rhode Island Secretary of State**	148 W River St, Providence, RI 02904	(401) 222-1487	https://www.sos.ri.gov/divisions/notary-public/apostilles-certifications/
South Carolina/ Columbia	**South Carolina Secretary of State**	1205 Pendleton St #525, Columbia, SC 29201	(803) 734-2512	https://sos.sc.gov/services-and-filings/apostilles
South Dakota/ Pierre	**South Dakota Secretary of State**	500 E Capitol Ave, Pierre, SD 57501	(605) 773-5004	https://sdsos.gov/general-services/apostilles-authentications.aspx
Tennessee/ Nashville	**Tennessee Secretary of State**	312 Rosa L Parks Ave, Nashville, TN 37243	(615) 741-0536	https://sos.tn.gov/businesses/guides/apostille-authentication-guide
Texas/Austin	**Texas Secretary of State**	PO Box 13550, Austin, Texas 78711	(512) 463-5705	https://www.sos.state.tx.us/authinfo.shtml

Immigration Resources in the US

Utah/Salt Lake City	**Utah Lieutenant Governor**	350 N State St #220, Salt Lake City, UT 84114	(801) 538-1041	https://authentications.utah.gov/process-from-home-page/
Vermont/ Montpelier	**Vermont Secretary of State**	1078 US Rte 2, Middlesex, Montpelier, VT 05633	(802) 828-3700	https://sos.vermont.gov/secretary-of-state-services/apostille-or-authentication/
Virginia/ Richmond	**Virginia Secretary of the Commonwealth**	1111 E Broad St, Richmond, VA 23219	(804) 692-0114	https://www.commonwealth.virginia.gov/official-documents/authentications/
Washington/ Olympia	**Washington Secretary of State**	PO Box 40228, Olympia, WA 98504	(360) 725-0377	https://www.sos.wa.gov/corps/apostilles/howtoobtainanapostilleorcertification.aspx
West Virginia/ Charleston	**West Virginia Secretary of State**	1900 Kanawha Blvd E, Bldg #1, #157-K ,Charleston, WV 25305	(304) 558-8000	https://sos.wv.gov/business/Pages/AuthDocs.aspx
Wisconsin/ Madison	**Wisconsin Secretary of State**	PO Box 7848, Madison WI 53707	(608) 266-8888	https://sos.wi.gov/apostilles.htm
Wyoming/ Cheyenne	**Wyoming Secretary of State**	122 W 25th St #100, Cheyenne, WY 82002	(307) 777-7370	https://sos.wyo.gov/services/authentication.aspx

Chicago Immigration Resources

Name	Address	Phone	Website (Spanish)	Description
Centro Romero	6216 North Clark, Chicago, IL 60660	(773) 508-5300	https://centroromero.org/legal-services/	Latin American Legal Assistance Services Program provides direct service representation, immigration education and advocacy services to low-income Spanish-speaking immigrants community members
National Immigrant Justice Center	224 S Michigan Ave #600, Chicago, IL 60604	(312) 660-1370	https://immigrantjustice.org	General immigration services, asylum, detained immigrants, human trafficking, LGBTQ immigrant, immigration court help desk, services for unaccompanied immigrant children

Chicago Immigration Resources

Name	Address	Phone	Website (Spanish)	Description
Chicago Legal Clinic	17 North State Street, Suite 1710, Chicago, IL 60602	(312) 726-2938	https://www.gclclaw.org/	Legal assistance including filings with USCIS, representation before the immigration court, representation before the Board of Immigration Appeals (BIA), federal court appeals. Areas of legal assistance include adjustment of status, asylum applications, DACA, employment-based immigrant petitions
Chicago Kent College of Law Immigration Clinic	565 W Adams St #600, Chicago, IL 60661	(312) 906-5366	https://kentlaw.iit.edu/law/clients-seeking-legal-services/c-k-law-group-practice-areas	Help completing forms, filings with USCIS, representation at asylum interviews, representation before immigration court and board of immigrant appeals
DePaul University College of Law Asylum and Immigration Clinic	25 E Jackson Blvd, Chicago, IL	(312) 362-8294	https://law.depaul.edu/academics/experiential-learning/legal-clinics/asylum-immigration/Pages/default.aspx	Help completing forms, filings with USCIS, representation at asylum interviews, representation before immigration court and board of immigrant appeals
Northwestern School of Law-- Bluhm Legal Clinic	375 E Chicago Ave, Chicago, IL 60611	(312) 503-8576	https://www.law.northwestern.edu/legalclinic/	Help completing forms, filings with USCIS, representation at asylum interviews, representation before the Immigration Court, representation before the Board of Immigration Appeals (BIA)
RefugeeOne	5707 N Lincoln Ave, Chicago, IL 60659	(773) 989-5647	https://www.refugeeone.org/	Help completing forms, filings with USCIS
Mil Mujeres Legal Services Chicago	222 S. Morgan Street, Suite 3B Chicago, IL 60607	(312) 219-2031	https://en.milmujeres.org/ (https://www.milmujeres.org)	Services for victims of domestic violence, provides direct legal services in the area of immigration law for Spanish speakers
National Immigrant Justice Center (Heartland Alliance)	224 S Michigan Ave #600, Chicago, IL 60604	(312) 660-1370	https://immigrantjustice.org/ (https://en.milmujeres.org/)	General immigration services, asylum, detained immigrants, human trafficking, LGBTQ immigrant, immigration court help desk, services for unaccompanied immigrant children

Immigration Resources in the US

Statewide / Multiple Location Immigration Resources

Name	Address	Phone	Website	Description
Spanish Community Center	309 N Eastern Ave, Joliet, IL 60432	(815) 727-3683	https://spanishcenter.org/	Help completing forms, filings with USCIS, representation at asylum interviews, representation before the immigration court, representation before the Board of Immigration Appeals (BIA), federal court appeals
Esperanza Legal Assistance Center	335 5th Ave Suite #207, Moline, IL 61265	(309) 732-0047		Help completing forms, filings with USCIS
Alliance for Immigrant Neighbors	382 S Mount Prospect Rd, Des Plaines, IL 60016	(224) 443-0113	https://www.allianceforimmigrants.org/	Legal services including adjustment of status, consular processing, DACA, employment authorization, family-based petitions, naturalization/citizenship
YMCA of the University of Illinois	1001 S Wright St, Champaign, IL 61820	(217) 417-5897	https://nawc.webflow.io/	Help completing forms, filings with USCIS
Northern Illinois Justice for Our Neighbors	Multiple Locations	(773) 609-4401	https://www.facebook.com/NIJFON/	Free high-quality legal services to low-income immigrants, engages in education and advocacy efforts. Staff and volunteers provide hospitality and childcare, assist with paperwork, and offer free legal consultations
Catholic Charities: Immigration & Naturalization Services Cook County	205 W Monroe, #200, Chicago, IL 60606	(312) 427-7078	https://www.catholiccharities.net/immigrant-refugee-and-legal-support/immigrant-services/	Adjustment of status, Consular processing, Deferred Action for Childhood Arrivals (DACA), Employment authorization, Family-based petitions, NACARA, Naturalization/Citizenship, T visas, Temporary Protected Status (TPS), U visas, Violence Against Women Act (VAWA) petitions
Illinois Coalition for Immigrant and Refugee Rights	228 S Wabash, Suite #800, Chicago, IL 60604	(312) 332-7360	https://www.icirr.org/	Healthcare access, immigrant family resource program, family support network and hotline, education and advocacy initiatives

Immigration Resources in the US

Statewide / Multiple Location Immigration Resources

Name	Address	Phone	Website	Description
The Immigration Project	211 Landmark Drive #B3A, Normal, IL 61761 and 505 W University Ave #214, Champaign, IL 61820	(309) 829-8703	https://www.immigrationproject.org/	Help completing forms, filings with USCIS, representation at asylum interviews, representation before the Immigration Court, representation before the Board of Immigration Appeals (BIA)
Catholic Charities of the Archdiocese of Chicago	721 N LaSalle Street, Chicago, Illinois 60654	(312) 655-7700	https://www.catholiccharities.net/immigrant-refugee-and-legal-support/immigrant-services/	Adjustment of status, Consular processing, Deferred Action for Childhood Arrivals (DACA), Employment authorization, Family-based petitions, NACARA, Naturalization/ Citizenship, T visas, Temporary Protected Status (TPS), U visas, Violence Against Women Act (VAWA) petitions
Catholic Charities: Immigration & Naturalization Services Lake County	671 S Lewis Ave, Waukegan, IL 60085	(847) 782-4225	https://www.catholiccharities.net/immigrant-refugee-and-legal-support/immigrant-services/	Adjustment of status, Consular processing, Deferred Action for Childhood Arrivals (DACA), Employment authorization, Family-based petitions, NACARA, Naturalization/ Citizenship, T visas, Temporary Protected Status (TPS), U visas, Violence Against Women Act (VAWA) petitions

Online Immigration Resources

Name	Website	Description
General Directory of Resources for Immigrants	https://www.immigrationadvocates.org/	Search for immigration legal services providers by state, county or detention facility. Only nonprofit organizations that provide free or low-cost immigration legal services are included
Legal Aid Online	https://www.illinoislegalaid.org/legal-information/us-citizenship	Legal aid tools to address issues such as deportation, unemployment, abuse, eviction, divorce, and debt. Their Form Library generates free legal papers for those seeking solutions to their legal problems. Multilingual

Mexico Resources

Mexican Consular Offices in the United States: Assists with getting your ID, ensuring your rights are protected in prison/detention, will help you find contact information for family members, help connect you with resources for health care and education			
State/City	Address	Phone/Email	Website
Arizona/ Yuma	298 S Main St, Yuma, AZ 85364	(928) 343-0066 conyuma@sre.gob.mx	https://consulmex.sre.gob.mx/yuma/
Arizona/ Tucson	3915 E Broadway Blvd, Tucson, AZ 85711	(520) 882-5595 contucmx@sre.gob.mx	https://consulmex.sre.gob.mx/tucson/
Arizona/ Nogales	135 W Cardwell St, Nogales, AZ 85621	(520) 287-2521 informacionnog@sre.gob.mx	https://consulmex.sre.gob.mx/nogales/
Arizona/ Phoenix	320 E McDowell Rd #320, Phoenix, AZ 85004	(602) 242-7398 conphoenix@sre.gob.mx	https://consulmex.sre.gob.mx/phoenix/
Arizona/ Douglas	1324 G Ave, Douglas, AZ 85607	(520) 364-3107 douglas@sre.gob.mx	https://consulmex.sre.gob.mx/douglas/
Arkansas/ Little Rock	3500 S University Ave, Little Rock, AR 72204	(501) 372-6933 consulmexlir@comcast.net	https://consulmex.sre.gob.mx/littlerock/
California/ Fresno	7435 N Ingram Ave, Fresno, CA 93711	(559) 233-3065 consulado@consulmexfrenso.net administracionfre01@sre.gob.mx informaticafre@sre.gob.mx	https://consulmex.sre.gob.mx/fresno/index.php/es/
California/ Calexico	408 Heber Ave, Caléxico, CA, 92231	(760) 357-3863 infocalexico@sre.gob.mx concalexico@sre.gob.mx	https://consulmex.sre.gob.mx/calexico/
California/ Oxnard	3151 W 5th St E-100, Oxnard, CA 93030	(805) 330-3060 consul@consulmexoxnard.com edelmoral@sre.gob.mx	https://consulmex.sre.gob.mx/oxnard/
California/ San Jose	302 Enzo Dr #200, San José, CA 95138	(424) 309-0009 consjose@sre.gob.mx	https://consulmex.sre.gob.mx/sanjose/
California/ San Francisco	532 Folsom St, San Francisco, CA 94105	(415) 354-1700 consfrancisco@sre.gob.mx	https://consulmex.sre.gob.mx/sanfrancisco/
California/ Santa Ana	2100 E 4th St, Santa Ana, CA 92705	(714) 253-3906 consana@sre.gob.mx	https://consulmex.sre.gob.mx/santaana/
California/ San Bernadino	293 N "D" St, San Bernadino, CA 92401	(909) 889-9836 consulmexsbd@sre.gob.mx	https://consulmex.sre.gob.mx/sanbernardino/
California/ Los Angeles	2401 W 6th St, Los Angeles, CA 90057	(213) 351-6800 lapublico@sre.gob.mx	https://consulmex.sre.gob.mx/losangeles/index.php/es/

Mexico Resources

California/ Sacramento	2093 Arena Blvd, Sacramento, CA 95834	(916) 536-6599 sacramento@sre.gob.mx	https://consulmex.sre.gob.mx/sacramento/
California/ San Diego	1549 India St, San Diego, CA 92101	(619) 231-8414 cgonzalezg@sre.gob.mx	https://consulmex.sre.gob.mx/sandiego/
Colorado/ Denver	5350 Leetsdale Dr, Denver, CO 80246	(303) 331-1110 infodenver@sre.gob.mx	https://consulmex.sre.gob.mx/denver/
Florida/ Orlando	2550 Technology Dr, Orlando, FL 32804	(407) 927-8297 consulado@conorlando.net jsabines@sre.gob.mx	https://consulmex.sre.gob.mx/orlando/
Florida/ Miami	1399 SW 1st Ave, Miami, FL 33130	(786) 268-4900 recepcionmia@sre.gob.mx	https://consulmex.sre.gob.mx/miami/
Georgia/ Atlanta	1700 Chantilly Dr NE, 30324	(404) 266-2233 conatlanta@sre.gob.mx	https://consulmex.sre.gob.mx/atlanta/
Idaho/ Boise	701 Morrison Knudsen Dr #102, Boise, ID 83712	(208) 343-6228 conboise@sre.gob.mx	https://consulmex.sre.gob.mx/boise/
Illinois/ Chicago	204 S Ashland Ave, Chicago, IL 60607	(312) 738-2383 conchicago@sre.gob.mx	https://consulmex.sre.gob.mx/chicago/
Indiana/ Inidianapolis	331 S East St, Indianapolis, IN 46204	(317) 761-7600 conindianapolis@sre.gob.mx indianapolis@sre.gob.mx	https://consulmex.sre.gob.mx/indianapolis/
Louisiana/ New Orleans	901 Convention Center Blvd #119, New Orleans, LA 70130	(504) 528-3722 connorleans@sre.gob.mx	https://consulmex.sre.gob.mx/nuevaorleans/
Massachusetts/ Boston	55 Franklin St, Boston, MA 02110	(617) 426-4181 cmxboston@sre.gob.mx	https://consulmex.sre.gob.mx/boston/
Michigan/ Detroit	1403 E 12 Mile Rd, Building E, Madison Heights, MI 48071	(248) 336-0320 detroit@sre.gob.mx	https://consulmex.sre.gob.mx/detroit/
Minnesota/ Saint Paul	797 E 7th St, Saint Paul, MN 55106	(651) 771-5494 conspaul@sre.gob.mx	https://consulmex.sre.gob.mx/saintpaul/
Missouri/ Kansas City	1617 Baltimore Ave, Kansas City, MO 64108	(816) 556-0800 conkansas@sre.gob.mx	https://consulmex.sre.gob.mx/kansascity/
Nebraska/ Omaha	7444 Farnam St, Omaha, NE 68114	(404) 266- 2233 conomaha@sre.gob.mx	https://consulmex.sre.gob.mx/omaha/
Nevada/ Las Vegas	823 S 6th St, Las Vegas, NV 89101	(702) 477-2700 conlvegas@sre.gob.mx	https://consulmex.sre.gob.mx/lasvegas/

Mexico Resources

New Mexico/ Albuquerque	1610 4th St NW, Albuquerque, NM 87102	(505) 247-2147 infoalb@sre.gob.mx	https://consulmex.sre.gob.mx/albuquerque/
New York/ New York	27 E 39th St, New York, NY 10016	(212) 217-6400 connyork@sre.gob.mx titularny@sre.gob.mx	https://consulmex.sre.gob.mx/nuevayork/index.php/espanol/
North Carolina/ Raleigh	431 Raleigh View Rd, Raleigh, NC 27610	(919) 615-3653 conraleigh@sre.gob.mx	https://consulmex.sre.gob.mx/raleigh/
Oregon/ Portland	1305 SW 12th Ave, Portland, OR 97201	(503) 274-1442 conportland@sre.gob.mx portland@sre.gob.mx	https://consulmex.sre.gob.mx/portland/
Pennsylvania/ Philadelphia	111 S Independence Mall E #310, Philadelphia, PA 19106	(215) 922-4262 confiladelfia@sre.gob.mx	https://consulmex.sre.gob.mx/filadelfia/
Puerto Rico/ San Juan	654 Ave Luis Muñoz Rivera #1110, San Juan, PR 00918	(787) 764-8923 consjuan@sre.gob.mx	https://consulmex.sre.gob.mx/sanjuan/
Texas/ Houston	10555 Richmond Ave, Houston, TX 77042	(713) 271-6800 conhouston@sre.gob.mx	https://consulmex.sre.gob.mx/houston/
Texas/ Del Rio	2207 N Bedell Ave, Del Río, TX 78840	(830) 775-2352 pvillasenor@sre.gob.mx	https://consulmex.sre.gob.mx/delrio/
Texas/ San Antonio	127 Navarro St, San Antonio, TX 78205	(210) 227 9145 info@consulmexsat.org	https://consulmex.sre.gob.mx/sanantonio/
Texas/ El Paso	910 E San Antonio Ave, El Paso, TX 79901	(915) 533 3644 conepaso@sre.gob.mx	https://consulmex.sre.gob.mx/elpaso/
Texas/ Dallas	1210 River Bend, Dallas, TX 75247	(214) 932-8670 infodallas@sre.gob.mx	https://consulmex.sre.gob.mx/dallas/
Texas/ Eagle Pass	2252 E Garrison St, Eagle Pass, TX 78852	(830) 773-9255 eaglepass@sre.gob.mx	https://consulmex.sre.gob.mx/eaglepass/
Texas/ McAllen	600 S Broadway St., McAllen, TX 78501	(956) 686-0243 conmallen@sre.gob.mx	https://consulmex.sre.gob.mx/mcallen/
Texas/ Austin	5202 E Ben White Blvd #150, Austin, TX 78741	(512) 478-2866 conaustin@sre.gob.mx	https://consulmex.sre.gob.mx/austin/
Texas/ Brownsville	301 México Blvd #F-2, Brownsville, TX 78520	(956) 542-4431 conbrownsville@sre.gob.mx	https://consulmex.sre.gob.mx/brownsville/
Texas/ Laredo	1612 Farragut St, Laredo, TX 78040	(956) 723-0990 informacionlar@sre.gob.mx	https://consulmex.sre.gob.mx/laredo/

Mexico Resources

Texas/ Presidio	319 W 21 De Marzo St, Presidio, TX 79845	(432)-229-2788 conpresidio@sre.gob.mx	https://consulmex.sre.gob.mx/presidio/
Utah/ Salt Lake City	660 S 200 E, #300, Salt Lake City, UT 84111	(801) 521-8502 atencionpublicosal@sre.gob.mx consuladoslc@consulmexslc.org	https://consulmex.sre.gob.mx/saltlakecity/
Washington/ Seattle	807 E Roy St, Seattle, WA 98102	(206) 448-3526 conseattle@sre.gob.mx	https://consulmex.sre.gob.mx/seattle/index.php/es/
Wisconsin/ Milwaukee	1443 N Prospect Ave, Milwaukee, WI 53202	(414) 944-7586, (414) 324 7643 conmilwaukee@sre.gob.mx	https://consulmex.sre.gob.mx/milwaukee/

Hotlines

Name	Phone	Website	Description
COVID-19 Hotline		https://coronavirus.gob.mx/contacto/	Call for information about COVID-19 if youhave symptoms of respiratory illness. Varies by state
National Helpline (Fundación Origin)	(555) 520 4427	www.origenac.org	Confidential psychological, medical and legal help. Hours: 8 AM- 10 PM
Suicide Hotline (International Bipolar Foundation)	(525) 510-2550	https://ibpf.org/resource/suicide-hotline-mexico/	Available 24 hours a day for help
National Life Hotline (Línea de la Vida)	(800) 911-2000	https://www.gob.mx/salud/prensa/014-linea-de-la-vida-ayuda-profesional-para-personas-con-depresion?fbclid=IwAR0I7z9La6q4030LujrW5FjZMyIRKl4279CZKrZwVL4BmWQZHncVSeXiGAI	Psychological assistance to people suffering depression, who might be at risk for suicide

Government Institutes

Name	Phone/Email	Website	Description
Civil Registry		https://embamex.sre.gob.mx/argentina/images/consular/ofregcivilenrepubmexic?fbclid=IwAR3MPgHmW10ZGN03nPJpIao1PSRcozaWyJ5eEl7u97veX0wUrkKy8Tclw_A	Birth, marriage, and death certificates
National Electoral Institute (INE)	(800) 433-2000	https://www.ine.mx/servicios-ine/	National ID card (INE)

Mexico Resources

Government Institutes

Name	Phone/Email	Website	Description
National Institute for Integral Family Development (DIF)	atencion_ ciudadana@dif. gob.mx	https://www.gob.mx/ difnacional	Food assistance (soup kitchen and food panrty), psychological assistance, legal support, home building materials, older adult community activities, community development support, stipends for people with disabilities, hearing aids (services vary by location)
Institute for Mexicans Abroad (IME)	(553) 686-5100	https://www.gob.mx/ime	Mexican government agency that supports Mexican citizens and others of Mexican descent who live and work in other countries (focused on US)
Institute of Health for Well-being (INSABI)	(800) 767-8527	https://www.gob.mx/insabi	List of public hospitals and clinics
Mexican Institute of Social Security (IMSS)	(800) 623-2323	http://www.imss.gob.mx/	Public hospital for workers at private companies
The Institute for Social Security Services for the Workers of the State (ISSSTE)	(555) 140-9617	https://www.gob.mx/issste	Public hospital for state workers
Secretary of Labor and Social Welfare (STPS)	(552) 000-5300	https://www.gob.mx/stps/	Job training and placement, worker protection
Tax Administration Service (SAT)	(556) 272-2728	https://www.sat.gob.mx/ home	Federal tax collection, new business registration
Secretary of Public Education (SEP)	(800) 288-6688	https://www.gob.mx/sep	Education at all levels, verification of US educational documents, English teacher positions
Secretary of Exterior Relations (SRE)		https://citas.sre.gob.mx/	Passports

Non-Profit Organizations

Name	Phone/Email	Website	Description
Comunidad en Retorno	info@comunida denretorno.com	https://www. comunidadenretorno.com/	A community of deported people defending the human rights of deported people and providing a network of support for their reintegration into the community

Directory

Mexico Resources

LGBTQ Resources

Name	Phone/Email	Address	Website
It Gets Better			https://itgetsbetter.org/mexico/
Human Rights Campaign: Equidad MX			https://www.hrc.org/press-releases/hrc-equidad-mx-global-workplace-equality-program-launches-in-mexico
Federación Mexicana de Empresarios LGBT	(556) 721-2138 contacto@fmelgbt.mx	Indianapolis 8-602B, Nápoles, Benito Juárez, 03810 Ciudad de México, CDMX, Mexico	https://www.facebook.com/fmelgbt/?locale=es_LA
Brújula Intersexual	brujulaintersexual@gmail.com		https://brujulaintersexual.org/
Racismo Mx	ayuda@racismo.mx		https://racismo.mx/

Mexico City Resources

GOVERNMENT INSTITUTES				
Name	Address	Phone/Email	Website	Description
Government of CDMX	Calle Plaza de la Constitución 1, Col Centro (Área 1), Alcaldía Cuauhtémoc, 06000		https://www.cdmx.gob.mx/	Job fairs, COVID-19 vaccine information, property tax payment
Civil Registry	Various Locations	(559) 179-6700	https://data.consejeria.cdmx.gob.mx/index.php/dgrc	Birth, marriage, and death certificates
National Electoral Institute (INE)	Various Locations	(800) 433-2000 inetelmx@ine.mx	https://app-inter.ife.org.mx/siac2011/citas_initCapturaCitas.siac	National ID card (INE)
Secretary of Public Education (SEP)	República de Argentina 28, Centro Histórico, 06020	(553) 601-7599	https://www.gob.mx/sep	Federal tax collection, new business registration
National Institute for Integral Family Development (DIF)	Ave San Francisco 1374, Col Tlacoquemécatl, Alcadía Benito Juárez, 03200	(555) 559-1919	https://www.dif.cdmx.gob.mx	A variety of services that include healthcare and food assistance, mental health and community services

Mexico Resources

Mexico City Resources

GOVERNMENT INSTITUTES				
Name	Address	Phone/Email	Website	Description
Institute of Health for Well-Being (INSABI)	Various Locations		https://www.gob.mx/insabi	List of public hospitals and clinics (with email contacts)
Mexican Institute of Social Security (IMSS)	Prol Lerdo 311, Tlatelolco, Cuauhtémoc, 06900		http://www.imss.gob.mx/directorio	Public hospital for workers at private companies
Secretary of Labor and Social Welfare (STPS)	Calzada San Antonio Abad 32, Col Tránsito, Cuauhtémoc, 06820	(555) 709-3233	www.trabajo.cdmx.gob.mx	Job training and placement, worker protection
Tax Administration Service (SAT)	Félix Cuevas 301, Col del Valle Sur, Benito Juárez, 03100	(556) 272- 2728	https://citas.sat.gob.mx/	Federal tax collection, new business registration
Secretary of Public Health (SEDESA)	Ave Insurgentes N, Conjunto Urbano #423, Col Nonoalco Tlatelolco, Alcaldía Cuauhtémoc, 06900	(555) 132-1250	https://www.salud.cdmx.gob.mx	Federal tax collection, new business registration
Secretary of Inclusion and Social Welfare	Calle Fernando de Alva Ixtlilxóchitl 185, Col Tránsito, Alcaldía Cuauhtémoc, 06820	(558) 957-3450	https://www.sibiso.cdmx.gob.mx	Implementing programs and policies for social development
Secretary of Foreign Relations (SRE)	Ave Juárez 20, Col Centro, Cuauhtémoc, Ciudad de México, 06010	(553) 686-5100	https://citas.sre.gob.mx/	Passport
ISSSTE Hospital General Tacuba	Lago Ontario 36, Tacuba, Miguel Hidalgo, 11410	(555) 399-6199	https://www.gob.mx/issste	Public hospital for state workers
Hospital Juárez de México	Ave Instituto Politécnico Nacional 5160, Magdalena de las Salinas, Delegación Gustavo A. Madero, 07760	(555) 747-7560	https://www.gob.mx/salud/hjm	Public hospital
Hospital General Gregorio Salas Flores	Calle del Carmen 42, Centro, Cuauhtémoc, 06020	(555) 702- 0372		Public hospital

Mexico Resources

Mexico City Resources

GOVERNMENT INSTITUTES				
Name	Address	Phone/Email	Website	Description
Comedor Comunitario CDMX	Calle Fernando de Alva Ixtlilxóchitl #185, Piso 3, Col Tránsito, Alcaldía Cuauhtémoc, 06820	(558) 957-3466	https://sibiso.cdmx.gob.mx/programa-comedores-sociales	Soup kitchen
NON-PROFIT ORGANIZATIONS				
Name	Address	Phone/Email	Website	Description
Tergar Meditation Community	Sultepec 35, Col Hipódromo Condesa, Delegación Cuauhtémoc	aprende@tergar.org	https://espanol.tergar.org/comunidades-y-grupos-de-practica/ciudad-de-mexico/	Meditation community
Comunidad en Retorno		info@comunidadenretorno.com	https://www.comunidadenretorno.com/	A community of deported people defending the human rights of deported people and providing a network of support for their reintegration into the community
Deportados Unidos en la Lucha		(557) 828-3480 anadeportadosunidosenlalucha.mx	https://deportadosunidosenlalucha.mx/	Referrals to community resources, accompaniment and orientation
New Comienzos	Plaza de la Republica 9, Tabacalera, Cuauhtémoc, 06030	(557) 733-1436 info@newcomienzos.org	www.newcomienzos.org	Resources to reintegrate into society, such as shelter, psychological help, employment
Directory of LGBTTTI Organizations			https://www.angloinfo.com/how-to/mexico/mexico-city/family/lgbt/lgbttti-organizations	
IDL Buró Legal	(554) 444-3923 info@idl.com.mx	Av de Las Fuentes 624 Jardines del Pedregal 01900 Mexico City, Mexico	https://idl.com.mx/en/home/	

Mexico Resources

Mexico City Resources

NON-PROFIT ORGANIZATIONS			
Name	Phone/Email	Address	Website
"Arturo Díaz Betancourt": Human Rights			http://www.letraese-ddhh.com/
Condesa Clinic	(555) 271-6133, (555) 271-6439	Gral Benjamín Hill 24, Hipódromo Condesa, Cuauhtémoc, 06170 Ciudad de México, CDMX, Mexico	https://condesa.cdmx.gob.mx/
Cuenta Conmigo	ConmigoMexico@gmail.com		https://www.facebook.com/ConmigoMexico/
Centro de Atención Integral de la Diversidad Sexual Tlalpan "Amélio Robles"	diversidadsexual.tlalpan@gmail.com		https://www.facebook.com/TlalpanLGBTI/
Centro Cultural de la Diversidad	(555) 514-2565	Colima #267, Roma Nte, Cuauhtémoc, 06700 Ciudad de México, CDMX, Mexico	https://www.forocafe.com.mx/
Asistencia Legal por los Derechos Humanos A. C. (ASILEGAL)	(555) 523-2690	C Pitágoras 920, Narvarte Poniente, Benito Juárez, 03020 Ciudad de México, CDMX, Mexico	https://asilegal.org.mx/
Casa de las Muñecas Tiresias, A. C.	(552) 227-1436 munecas.tiresias@gmail.com		https://www.munecastiresias.org/
Centro de Apoyo a las Identidades Trans, AC	(552) 753-8095		https://cait.org.mx/
National Commission on Human Rights	(555) 448-8988	Oklahoma 133, Nápoles, Benito Juárez, 03810 Ciudad de México, CDMX, Mexico	https://www.cndh.org.mx/
Consejo Nacional Para Prevenir la Discriminación	(555) 262-1490	Londres 247, Juárez, Cuauhtémoc, 06600 Ciudad de México, CDMX, Mexico	https://www.conapred.org.mx/
Council to Prevent and Eliminate Discrimination in Mexico City	(555) 341-3010	Calle Gral Prim 10, Colonia Centro, Centro, Cuauhtémoc, 06000 Centro, CDMX, Mexico	https://www.copred.cdmx.gob.mx/

Mexico Resources

Mexico City Resources

NON-PROFIT ORGANIZATIONS			
Name	Phone/Email	Address	Website
Covenant House (Casa Alianza) Mexico	(800) 388-3888 mexico@casa-alianzamexico.org	Moctezuma #68 Col Guerrero, Alcaldía Cuauhtémoc México CDMX. CP. 06300	https://www.covenanthouse.org/camino
México Vivo	(555) 615-7383 fundacion@mexicovivo.org	Bajío #295, Col. Roma Sur, Municipio Cuauhtémoc, CDMX, C.P. 06760	https://mexicovivo.org/
Yaaj México	(557) 031-3895	C. Monte Albán 6, Narvarte Oriente, Benito Juárez, 03020 Ciudad de México, CDMX, Mexico	https://www.yaajmexico.org/
Casa Frida Refugio LGBT	(558) 926-0663 casafrida@refugiolgbt.org	Calle, C. Sur 105 434, Héroes de Churubusco, Iztapalapa, 09090 Ciudad de México, CDMX, Mexico	https://www.refugiocasafrida.com/

Matamoros, Tamaulipas

GOVERNMENT INSTITUTES				
Name	Address	Phone/Email	Website	Description
Government of Matamoros	Sexto S/N, González y Morelos, Centro Heroica	(868) 810-8000 contacto@matamoros.gob.mx	https://www.matamoros.gob.mx	Job fairs, COVID-19 vaccine information, property tax payment
Civil Registry	Various Locations	(868) 812-3431	https://consulmex.sre.gob.mx/reinounido/index.php/en/contenido/5-registro-civil/198-register-offices	Birth, marriage, and death certificates

Matamoros, Tamaulipas

GOVERNMENT INSTITUTES				
Name	Address	Phone/Email	Website	Description
National Electoral Institute (INE)	Various Locations	(800) 433-2000	https://app-inter.ife.org.mx/siac2011/citas_initCapturaCitas.siac	National ID card (INE)
Tamaulipas State Governent	15 y 16 Juárez-Palacio de Gobierno, 3er Piso Cd Victoria, 87000	(834) 318-8000	https://www.tamaulipas.gob.mx	Driver's license
Secretary of Public Education (SEP)	Calz Gral. Luis Caballero S/N, Fracc. Las Flores, Cd Victoria, 87078	(834) 318-6600	https://www.tamaulipas.gob.mx/educacion/	Education at all levels, verification of US educational documents, English teacher positions
National Institute for Integral Family Development (DIF)	Calle 4a y Camilo Manzo S/N Col Lucero, 87350	(868) 810-9550	https://www.difmatamoros.gob.mx	A variety of services that include healthcare and food assistance, mental health and community services
Institute of Health for Well-Being (INSABI)	Ave Francisco I Madero Np. 414, Zona Centro, Ciudad Victoria, 87000	(834) 318-6300	https://www.tamaulipas.gob.mx/salud/infraestructura-en-salud/hospitales-generales/	List of public hospitals and clinics
Hospital General Altamira	Carretera Tampico-Mante Km 27, 89603	(833) 331-9837		Public hospital
Hospital General Mante	Calle Sabino 300 Ote Col, Altavista, 89980	(831) 233-8160		Public hospital
IMSS General Hospital of Zone 13	Sexta Ocampo 800, Zona Centro, 87300	(868) 812-2391	http://www.imss.gob.mx	Public hospital for workers at private companies
The Institute for Social Security Services for the Workers of the State (ISSSTE)	Calle Canales 103, Lázaro Cárdenas, 87410	(868) 812-4150	https://www.gob.mx/issste	Public hospital for state workers

Mexico Resources

Matamoros, Tamaulipas

GOVERNMENT INSTITUTES				
Name	Address	Phone/Email	Website	Description
Tax Administration Service (SAT)	Prol C Calixto Ayala 202, Industrial, 87350	(868) 811-0200	https://citas.sat.gob.mx/	Federal tax collection, new business registration
Secretary of Labor and Social Welfare (STPS)			https://www.tamaulipas.gob.mx/trabajo/#	Job training and placement, worker protection
Secretary of Foreign Relations (SRE)	C Miguel Saenz S/N, Jardín, 87330	(834) 172-5650	https://citas.sre.gob.mx/	Passport
Tamaulipeca Women's Institute	Ave Constitución S/N	(868) 812-5140	https://www.tamaulipas.gob.mx/mujeres/	Support for women experiencing: violence and education, social work, legal assistance, and training for women
Tamulipas Insitute for Migrants	Calle Bravo 2123, Sector Centro, Nuevo Laredo, 88000	(867) 712- 3380		Provides support and care for returnees, including food and shelter

NON-PROFIT ORGANIZATIONS				
Name	Address	Phone	Website	Description
San Juan Diego and Francisco de Asís Shelter	Ave. Golfo de Mexico 48, Col. Ampliación Solidaridad, 87456	(868) 822-2213 (868) 822-4689	https://redes.dh.tamu.edu/node/56	Support for migrants who travel through Mexico or who have returned to the country

Reynosa, Tamaulipas

GOVERNMENT INSTITUTES				
Name	Address	Phone/Email	Website	Description
Government of Reynosa	Morelos 645, Entre Hidalgo y Juárez, 88500	(899) 932-3200 direcciondesistemas@reynosa.gob.mx	https://www.reynosa.gob.mx	Job fairs, COVID-19 vaccine information, property tax payment
Civil Registry	Various Locations		https://consulmex.sre.gob.mx/reinounido/index.php/en/contenido/5-registro-civil/198-register-offices	Birth, marriage, and death certificates
National Electoral Institute (INE)	Various Locations	(800) 433-2000	https://app-inter.ife.org.mx/siac2011/citas_initCapturaCitas.siac	National ID card (INE)
Tamaulipas State Government	15 y 16 Juárez, Palacio de Gobierno, 3er Piso, Cd Victoria, 87000	(834) 318-8000	https://www.tamaulipas.gob.mx	Driver's license
Secretary of Public Education (SEP)	Calz Gral Luis Caballero S/N, Fracc Las Flores, 87078	(834) 318-6655	https://www.tamaulipas.gob.mx/educacion/	Education at all levels, verification of US educational documents, English teacher positions
National Institute for Integral Family Development (DIF)	Morelos 645, Entre Hidalgo y Juárez, 88500	(899) 925-3614 direcciondesistemas@reynosa.gob.mx	http://www.difreynosa.gob.mx	A variety of services that include healthcare and food assistance, mental health and community services
Institute of Health for Well-Being (INSABI)	Various Locations	(800) 767- 8527	https://www.tamaulipas.gob.mx/salud/infraestructura-en-salud/hospitales-generales/ or https://www.gob.mx/insabi	List of public hospitals and clinics
Mexican Institute of Social Security (IMSS)	Various Locations		http://www.imss.gob.mx/directorio/?page=730	Public hospital for workers at private companies

Mexico Resources

Reynosa, Tamaulipas

GOVERNMENT INSTITUTES				
Name	Address	Phone/Email	Website	Description
The Institute for Social Security Services for the Workers of the State (ISSSTE)	Calle Nicolás Bravo S/N, Ferrocarril Zona Centro, 88500	(899) 922-2690	https://www.gob.mx/issste	Public hospital for state workers
Tax Administration Service (SAT)	José María Morelos S/N, Rodríguez, 88631	(556) 272-2728	https://citas.sat.gob.mx/	Federal tax collection, new business registration
Secretary of Foreign Relations (SRE)	Ocampo 1005, 88500	(800) 801-0773	https://citas.sre.gob.mx/	Passport
NON-PROFIT ORGANIZATIONS				
Name	Address	Phone/Email	Website	Description
Casa del Migrante	Nogal-Aldama 501, Col Aquiles Serdan I, 88520	(656) 551 641 casamigrantetkt@hotmail.com	https://www.facebook.comCasa-Del-Migrante-de-Nuestra-Señora-de-Guadalupe-1608050076131147/	Migrant shelter

Ciudad Juárez, Chihuahua

GOVERNMENT INSTITUTES				
Name	Address	Phone	Website	Description
Government of Ciudad Juárez	Ave Francisco Villa 950 N, Centro, 32000	(656) 737-0000	http://www.juarez.gob.mx/	Job fairs, COVID-19 vaccine information, property tax payment
Civil Registry	Various Locations		https://www.chihuahua.gob.mx/registrocivil	Birth, marriage, and death certificates

Ciudad Juárez, Chihuahua

GOVERNMENT INSTITUTES				
Name	Address	Phone	Website	Description
National Electoral Institute (INE)	Ave Tecnologico 4902, Abraham González, 31104	(614) 440-0809	https://app-inter.ife.org.mx/siac2011/citas_initCapturaCitas.siac	National ID card (INE)
Chihuahua State Government			http://www.chihuahua.gob.mx	Driver's license
Secretary of Public Education (SEP)	José Luis Revilla 440, Constitución, 32260	(656) 629-3300	http://educacion.chihuahua.gob.mx/secciones/juarez	Education at all levels, verification of US educational documents, English teacher positions
National Institute for Integral Family Development (DIF)	Ave Tecnológico 2903, col Magisterial Chihuahua, 31310	(614) 214-4000	https://difchihuahua.gob.mx	A variety of services that include healthcare and food assistance, mental health and community services
Hospital General de Ciudad Juárez	Ave Paseo Triunfo de la República 2404, Partido Escobedo, 32330	(656) 173-0700		Public hospital
Central Hospital Universario	Antonio Rosales #33000, Col Obrera, 31350	(614) 180-0800		Public hospital
Mexican Institute of Social Security (IMSS)	Various Locations		http://www.imss.gob.mx/directorio/?page=474	Public hospital for workers at private companies
Hospital General de Zona ISSSTE	Anillo Envolvente del Pronaf, Zona Pronaf Condominio La Plata, 32315	(656) 613-0081	https://www.gob.mx/issste	Public hospital for state workers
Tax Administration Service (SAT)	Ave Teófilo Borunda 8670-A, Partido Iglesias, 32528	(556) 272-2728	https://citas.sat.gob.mx/	Federal tax collection, new business registration
Secretary of Foreign Relations (SRE)	Eje Juan Gabriel 109	(656) 962-6101	https://citas.sre.gob.mx/	Passport

Mexico Resources

NON-PROFIT ORGANIZATIONS				
Name	Address	Phone/Email	Website	Description
Soup Kitchen	Calle Garambullo 7130, Héroes de la Revolución, 32696	(656) 667-7184		
Casa del Migrante en Juárez, A.C.	Calle Neptuno #1855, Col Satelite, 32540	(656) 687-0676 ivonnedj105245 @yahoo.com.mx	https://m.facebook.comCasaDelMigranteEnJuarezAC/	Shelter for migrants
Uno de Siete Migrando (Casa del Migrante Chihuahua)	Calle Ciudad Camargo 101, Col Revolucion, 31135	(614) 688-2842 comunicacion1de7@gmail.com	http://www.unodesietemigrando.org.mx	Shelter for migrants
Deported Veterans Support House-Juarez Bunker		(656) 656-7839 panchito251144 @gmail.com	https://web.facebook.com/DVSHJuarez/?_rdc=1&_rdr	Assistance with, food, clothing, shelter, job training, psychological and legal resources, and advocacy

Tijuana, Baja California

GOVERNMENT INSTITUTES				
Name	Address	Phone/Email	Website	Description
Government of Tijuana	Ave Independencia 1350, Zona Urbana Río, 22010	(664) 973-7000	https://www.tijuana.gob.mx/	Job fairs, COVID-19 vaccine information, property tax payment
Civil Registry	Various Locations		https://www.tijuana.gob.mx/dependencias/RegistroCivil/index.aspx	Birth, marriage, and death certificates
National Electoral Institute (INE)	Various Locations	(800) 433-2000 inetelmx@ine.mx	https://app-inter.ife.org.mx/siac2011/citas_initCapturaCitas.siac	National ID card (INE)

Mexico Resources

Tijuana, Baja California

GOVERNMENT INSTITUTES				
Name	Address	Phone/Email	Website	Description
Baja California State Government	Vía Oriente 10252, Zona del Río, 22320	(664) 624-2000	https://www.bajacalifornia.gob.mx/	Driver's license
Secretary of Public Education (SEP)	Ave Independencia 1350, Zona Urbana Río, 22010	(664) 973-7258	https://sepm.tijuana.gob.mx/	Education at all levels, verification of US educational documents, English teacher positions
National Institute for Integral Family Development (DIF)	Blvd Insurgentes #1760-8, Fracc Los Alamos, 22110	(664) 608-8200	https://dif.tijuana.gob.mx/#	A variety of services that include healthcare and food assistance, mental health and community services
Institute of Health for Well-Being (INSABI)	Various Locations		https://www.saludbc.gob.mx/pages/pdf/directorio.pdf	List of public hospitals and clinics
General Hospital of Tijuana	Ave Centenario #10851, Zona Río, 22010	(664) 684-0080	https://www.facebook.com/hospital.general.tijuana	Public hospital
IMSS of Tijuana	Blvd Agua Caliente 10610, Aviación, 22420	(664) 629-6300	http://www.imss.gob.mx/	Public hospital for workers at private companies
ISSSTE Hospital General Fray Junipero Serra	Ave las Palmas 4141, 20 de Noviembre, 22100	(664) 681-4386	https://www.gob.mx/issste	Public hospital for state workers
Tax Administration Service (SAT)	Fuerza Aerea Mexicana S/N, primera sur Edificio, Centro Urbano 70-76, 22410	(556) 272-2728	https://citas.sat.gob.mx/	Federal tax collection, new business registration
Secretary of Foreign Relations (SRE)	Ave Paseo de los Héroes 9111, Zona Centro, 22010	(800) 801-0773	https://citas.sre.gob.mx/	Passport

Mexico Resources

NON-PROFIT ORGANIZATIONS				
Name	Address	Phone/Email	Website	Description
Casa del Migrante en Tijuana	Galileo St #239, Col Postal, 22416	(664) 382-7685, (664) 682-5180 casadelmigrantetijuana@gmail.com	https://casadelmigrantetijuana.com/	Migrant shelter, medical care, document and employment help
Casa Madre Assunta	Galileo 2305, Col Postal 22416	(664) 683-0575, (664) 577-0025 centromadreasunta@gmail.com	http://institutomadreasunta.com.mx/	Congregation supporting welfare and care programs for migrants
Enclave Caracol	8220 Calle 1ra, Zona Centro, 22000	(664) 379-1818 enclavecaracol@gmail.com	www.enclavecaracol.wordpress.com	Social space in downtown Tijuana used for community gatherings and events
Espacio Migrante	Calle Aldrete 911, Col Zona Norte	espaciomigrante@gmail.com	www.espaciomigrante.org	Support for migrants, refugees, and asylum seekers
Dreamers' Moms		(754) 234-6924 dreamersmom2012@gmail.com	https://web.facebook.com/DREAMers Moms	National movement of women and moms for fair immigration reform
YMCA House for Minor Migrants	Blvd Cuauhtémoc Sur 3170, Col Chulavista, 22045	(664) 686-1359 casasymca@pymcadescom.org.mx	https://www.facebook.com/profile.php?id=100081558090834	Support for minors who have been deported
Deported Veteran Support House	Juan Álvarez 1821, Tomás Aquino, 22414	(626) 569-5491 banishedveteran@yahoo.com	https://web.facebook.com/DeportedVeteransSupportHousePage/?_rdc=1&_rdr	Food, clothing, and shelter for deported veterans
Al Otro Lado de Tijuana	511 E San Ysidro Blvd # 333, San Ysidro, CA 92173	(664) 208-8994 info@alotrolado.org	https://alotrolado.org/	Holistic legal and humanitarian support to refugees, deportees, and other migrants in the US and Tijuana
Comunidad Cultural de Tijuana LGBTI, A. C. (COCUT LGBTI A.C.)	Puente México 8202, Zona Centro, 22000 Tijuana, B.C., Mexico	(664) 290-9007 cocut2010@hotmail.com	https://www.facebook.com/cocutlgbti/	

Nogales, Sonora

GOVERNMENT INSTITUTES				
Name	Address	Phone/Email	Website	Description
Government of Nogales	Ave Obregón #339, Col. Centro	(631) 162-5000	https://nogalessonora.gob.mx	Job fairs, COVID-19 vaccine information, property tax payment
Civil Registry	Various Locations		https://www.registrolegal.es/registro-civil/nogales	Birth, marriage, and death certificates
National Electoral Institute (INE)	Various Locations		https://app-inter.ife.org.mx/siac2011/citas_initCapturaCitas.siac	National ID card (INE)
Sonora State Government	Comonfort y Dr Paliza S/N, Colonia Centenario, Hermosillo, 83260	(662) 108-4300	https://www.sonora.gob.mx	Driver's license
Secretary of Public Education (SEP)	Paseo Real del Arco y Paseo Alegre S/N, Fracc Paseo del Sol, 83246	delegacion.son@nube.sep.gob.mx	https://www.gob.mx/sep/acciones-y-programas/sonora-79625	Education at all levels, verification of US educational documents, English teacher positions
National Institute for Integral Family Development (DIF)	Blvd El Greco S/N, El Greco, 84066	(631) 162- 3210	https://difnogales.webcindario.com/	A variety of services that include healthcare and food assistance, mental health and community services
Institute of Health for Well-Being (INSABI)	Centro de Gobierno, Edificio Sonora, Primer Nivel Norte, Blvd Paseo Río Sonora y Comonfort, C.P. Hermosillo, Sonora	(662) 108-4500	http://www.saludsonora.gob.mx	List of public hospitals and clinics
Hospital General Nogales	Dr Francisco Arreola 1277, Moderna, 84055	(631) 313-3465	https://twitter.com/ssaludsonora	Public hospital

Mexico Resources

Nogales, Sonora

GOVERNMENT INSTITUTES				
Name	Address	Phone/Email	Website	Description
Mexican Institute of Social Security (IMSS)	Ave Obregón 756 esq, Gral Mariano Escobedo, Centro, 84000	(631) 313-5915	http://www.imss.gob.mx/directorio/?page=672	Public hospital for workers at private companies
ISSSTE Clinica Hospital Nogales	Blvd del Ensueño, Lomas de Fátima, 84020	(631) 299-9888	https://www.gob.mx/issste	Public hospital for state workers
Tax Administration Service (SAT)	Avr Nuevo Nogales 2587, Industrial, 84094	(631) 311-0302	https://citas.sat.gob.mx/	Federal tax collection, new business registration
Secretary of Foreign Relations (SRE)	Various Locations		https://citas.sre.gob.mx/	Passport

NON-PROFIT ORGANIZATIONS				
Name	Address	Phone/Email	Website	Description
Shelter for Migrant Minors	Boulevard San Carlos, esq con Santa Catalina, Fracc San Carlos III Etapa	(631) 209-5724 juridiconogales@difson.gob.mx		Migrant shelter
HEPAC (Casa de la misericordia de todas las naciones)	Calle Los Tigres 160, Bella Vista, 84046	(333) 141-6021 team@hepacnogales.org	https://www.facebook.com/HEPACMX/	Migrant advocacy
KINO Border Initiative	Edificio 3, Dept 401 Col Fovissste II, 84020	(631) 316-2086	www.kinoborderinitiative.org/es/	Migrant shelter

Mexico Resources

Hermosillo, Sonora

GOVERNMENT INSTITUTES				
Name	Address	Phone	Website	Description
Government of Hermosillo	Blvd. Hidalgo y Comonfort, Col Centenario, 83260	(662) 289-3000	https://www.hermosillo.gob.mx	Job fairs, COVID-19 vaccine information, property tax payment
Civil Registry	Various Locations	(662) 289-6600	https://consulmex.sre.gob.mx/reinounido/index.php/en/contenido/5-registro-civil/198-register-offices-in-mexico	Birth, marriage, and death certificates
National Electoral Institute (INE)	Various Locations	(662) 213-0870	https://app-inter.ife.org.mx/siac2011/citas_initCapturaCitas.siac	National ID card (INE)
Sonora State Government	Comonfort y Dr Paliza S/N, Colonia Centenario, C.P. 83260	(662) 108-4300	https://www.sonora.gob.mx/	Driver's license
Secretary of Public Education (SEP)	Blvd Luis Donaldo Colosio, Col Las Quintas, 83240	(662) 289-7600	https://www.sec.gob.mx/	Education at all levels, verifications of US educational documents, English teacher positions
National Institute for Integral Family Development (DIF)	Blvd Hidalgo y Comonfort Col Centenario	(662) 289-3000	http://web.difson.gob.mx/	A variety of services that include healthcare and food assistance, mental health and community services
Institute of Health for Well-Being (INSABI)	Various Locations	(662) 212-4045	http://www.saludsonora.gob.mx	List of public hospitals and clinics
Hospital General del Estado de Sonora (IMSS)	Blvd Luis Encinas J S/N, San Benito, 83000	(662) 259-2500	https://www.facebook.com/hospitalgeneralsonora	Public hospital for workers at private companies
ISSSTE Hospital General Zona 2 Hermosillo	Calle Benito Juárez 206, Modelo, 83190	(662) 214-1415	http://www.imss.gob.mx/directorio/?page=672	Public hospital for state workers

Mexico Resources

Hermosillo, Sonora

GOVERNMENT INSTITUTES				
Name	Address	Phone	Website	Description
Family Medicine Clinic ISSSTE	Blvd Morelos y, Ave Cuatro S/N, 83140	(662) 211- 2732	https://www.gob.mx/issste	Public hospital for state workers
Tax Administration Service (SAT)	Paseo Río Sonora Sur S/N, Villa de Seris, 83280	(556) 272-2728	https://citas.sat.gob.mx/	Federal tax collection, new business registration
Secretary of Foreign Relations (SRE)	Comonfort S/N, Proyecto Rio Sonora, 83270	(553) 686-5581	https://citas.sre.gob.mx/	Passport

Cancún, Quintana Roo

GOVERNMENT INSTITUTES				
Name	Address	Phone/Email	Website	Description
Cancún City Government	Palacio Municipal, Ave Tulum No. 5 Sm. 5, Benito Juárez, 77500	(998) 881-2800	https://cancun.gob.mx/	Job fairs, COVID-19 vaccine information, property tax payment
Civil Registry	Various Locations	(983) 832-8521	https://cancun.gob.mx/	Birth, marriage and death certificates
National Electoral Institute (INE)	Various Locations	(800) 433-2000	www.ine.mx/	National ID card (INE)
Secretaria Municipal de Seguridad Pública y Tránsito	Ave Xcaret con Ave La Costa, Sm. 21, Mz. 8, lote 13, 77500	(998) 283-2070 smspyt@smspyt.cancun.gob.mx	https://cancun.gob.mx/ayuntamiento/organigrama/secretaria-municipal-de-seguridad-publica-y-transito/	Driver's license

Cancún, Quintana Roo

GOVERNMENT INSTITUTES				
Name	Address	Phone/Email	Website	Description
Secretary of Public Education (SEP)	Av Insurgentes, Gonzalo Guerrero, Chetumal, 77020	(983) 835-1350	https://qroo.gob.mx/seq/	Education at all levels, verification of US educational documents, English teacher positions
National Institute for Integral Family Development (DIF)	Calle 44 Pte, Manzana 76, Reg. 94	(998) 888-8921	http://difbenitojuarez.gob.mx/	A variety of services that include healthcare and food assistance, mental health and community services
Institute of Health for Well-Being (INSABI)	Various Locations		https://www.gob.mx/insabi	List of public hospitals and clinics
Mexican Institute of Social Security (IMSS)	Av Coba S/N Supermanzana 22 Centro, 77500	(998) 884-1919	www.imss.gob.mx	Public hospital for workers at private companies
The Institute for Social Security Services for the Workers of the State (ISSSTE)	Libramiento Av Kabah Region 93, C. 93, Col. Centro, 77517	(998) 888-7261	https://www.gob.mx/issste	Public hospital for state workers
Tax Administration Service (SAT)	Av Bonampak s/n Mz 1 Lte 4 y 5 locales 8-10, 8, 77500	(556) 272-2728	https://citas.sat.gob.mx/	Federal tax collection, new business registration
Secretary of Foreign Relations (SRE)	Ave Carlos J. Nader SM 5 Mz.8 Lt.2, Centro, 77500	(998) 272-2639	https://citas.sre.gob.mx/	Passport
Secretary of Labor and Employment (STPS)	Av Efrain Aguilar Número 467, Campestre, Chetumal, 77030	(983) 835-1350	https://qroo.gob.mx/styps/	Job training and placement, worker protection

Mexico Resources

Cancún, Quintana Roo

NON-PROFIT ORGANIZATIONS				
Name	Address	Phone/Email	Website	Description
El Centro Integral de Atención a las Mujeres (CIAM)	Av Miguel Hidalgo, Manzana 63, Lote 1, Supermanzana 103, 77539	(998) 898-0755 comunicacion@ciamcancun.com	https://www.ciamcancun.org/	Peace and non-violence education, conflict resolution
Colectivo para el Impacto Social	Zona Zentro 3er piso, SM 13. Mza.1. Lt 22. Loc. 14-16	(998) 254-6500 fundacionrcd@rcdhotels.com	https://rcdfundacion.org/home/	Provides equal opportunities to citizens through education, health, and social development

San Miguel de Allende, Guanajuato

GOVERNMENT INSTITUTES				
Name	Address	Phone/Email	Website	Description
San Miguel de Allende City Government	Bulevar de la Conspiración 130, Salida a Querétaro	(415) 152-9600	https://sanmigueldeallende.gob.mx/	Job fairs, property tax payment
Civil Registry	Salida a Querétaro Kilómetro 1, Centro, 37748	(415) 152-2042 contacto@guanajuato.gob.mx	https://sg.guanajuato.gob.mx/index.php/registro-civil/	Birth, marriage and death certificates
National Electoral Institute (INE)	Plaza Real del Conde, Paseo de los Conspiradores 2, Local 19 AB, Zona Centro, 37700	(415) 152-3565	https://app-inter.ife.org.mx/siac2011/citas_initCapturaCitas.siac	National ID card (INE)
Guanajuato State Government	Paseo de la Presa 103, 36000	(800) 465-2486	https://www.guanajuato.gob.mx/	Driver's license
Secretary of Public Education (SEP)			https://www.gob.mx/sep	Education at all levels, verification of US educational documents, English teacher positions

San Miguel de Allende, Guanajuato

GOVERNMENT INSTITUTES				
Name	Address	Phone/Email	Website	Description
National Institute for Integral Family Development (DIF)	San Antonio Abad S/N, Centro, 37700	(415) 152-0910	http://difsanmigueldeallende.gob.mx/programas-2/alimentario/	A variety of services that include healthcare and food assistance, mental health and community services
Institute of Health for Well-Being (INSABI)	Various Locations		https://salud.guanajuato.gob.mx/Directorio-Unidades-Medicas.php	List of public hospitals and clinics
Caises San Miguel de Allende	Av Arcoiris S/N, Fracc La Lejona 2a, 37736	(415) 152-6210 modulosugsma@gmail.com	https://www.facebook.com/caisessma/	Public hospital
Hospital General San Miguel de Allende "Felipe G. Dobarganes"	Ave 1 De Mayo N° 7, Fracc Ignacio Ramirez, 37748	(415) 120-4746		Public hospital
Mexican Institute of Social Security (IMSS)	Calz de La Aurora S/N, Aurora, 37715	(415) 152-0699	http://www.imss.gob.mx/	Public hospital for workers at private companies
The Institute for Social Security Services for the Workers of the State (ISSSTE)	Francisco José de Landeta 1	(415) 152-5181		Public hospital for state workers
Tax Administration Service (SAT)	Ave de la Conspiración 302, Local BB03 y BB04, Col. El Deportivo, 37748	(556) 272-2728	https://citas.sat.gob.mx/	Federal tax collection, new business registration
Secretary of Foreign Relations (SRE)	Blvd de la Conspiración 130, 37748	(415) 110-3017	https://citas.sre.gob.mx/	Passport

Mexico Resources

Leon, Guanajuato

GOVERNMENT INSTITUTES				
Name	Address	Phone/Email	Website	Description
Government of León	Plaza Principal S/N, Centro Histórico León, 37000		https://www.leon.gob.mx/	Job fairs, COVID-19 vaccine information, property tax payment
Civil Registry	Various Locations	(800) 465-2486 contacto@guanajuato.gob.mx	https://segob.guanajuato.gob.mx/AgendaServiciosRC/Agendar/index.php	Birth, marriage, and death certificates
National Electoral Institute (INE)	Ave del Astillero 148, Centro Bodeguero las Trojes, 37227	(477) 776-5900	https://app-inter.ife.org.mx/siac2011/citas_initCapturaCitas.siac	National ID card (INE)
Guanajuato State Government	Paseo de la Presa 103, 36000	(800) 465-2486	https://www.guanajuato.gob.mx/	Driver's license
Secretary of Public Education (SEP)	Conjunto Administrativo, Pozuelos S/N	(473) 735-1000	https://www.seg.guanajuato.gob.mx/SitePages/Home.aspx	Education at all levels, verification of US educational documents, English teacher positions
National Institute for Integral Family Development (DIF)	Plaza Revolución 107, Col San Juan de Dios, 37004	(447) 215-6300 angeles.franco@leon.gob.mx	https://dif.leon.gob.mx/	A variety of services that include healthcare and food assistance, mental health and community services
Institute of Health for Well-Being (INSABI)		(477) 719-7400	https://salud.guanajuato.gob.mx/	Public hospital
Nuevo Hospital General de León	Blvd Milenio 1002, Fracciones de los Aguirre, 37672	(477) 719-7400	https://salud.guanajuato.gob.mx	Public hospital
Hospital Angeles León	Ave Cerro Gordo, Lomas del Campestre, 37150	(477) 788-5600	https://hospitalesangeles.com/leon/	Public hospital
State Delegation of IMSS in Guanajuato	Blvd Adolfo López Mateos S/N, Los Paraisos, 37320	(477) 717-4000	http://www.imss.gob.mx/directorio/?page=556	Public hospital for workers at private companies

Mexico Resources

Leon, Guanajuato

GOVERNMENT INSTITUTES				
Name	Address	Phone/Email	Website	Description
The Institute for Social Security Services for the Workers of the State (ISSSTE)	Calle Cholula 305, Azteca, 37520	(554) 000-1000 atencionciudadana@issste.gob.mx	https://www.gob.mx/issste	Public hospital for state workers
Tax Administration Service (SAT)	Blvd Campestre 55, Col. La Florida, 37190	(556) 272-2728	https://citas.sat.gob.mx/	Federal tax collection, new business registration
Secretary of Labor and Social Welfare		(800) 465-2486	http://sg.guanajuato.gob.mx/sstps/	Job training and placement, worker protection
Secretary of Foreign Relations (SRE)	Plaza Galería Las Torres, Blvd Juan Alonso de Torres Oriente 1315, Col San José del Consuelo, 37200	(477) 215-0203	https://citas.sre.gob.mx/	Passport

NON-PROFIT ORGANIZATIONS				
Name	Address	Phone/Email	Website	Description
Fundación León	Blvd Mariano Escobedo 5604 A Pte, Across from Escuela Tecnica 53	(477) 762-1749	http://www.fundacionleon.org.mx/en-us/home.aspx	Community center
Casa del Migrante Galilea	Calle Río Balsas 211, San Miguel, 37390	(477) 715-5074 casa.migrante.galilea@gmail.com	https://casagalileamigrante.godaddysites.com/	Migrant shelter
Casa del Migrante Manos Extendidas	16 de Septiembre 430, Barrio del Zapote 38057	(461) 334-9644 manosalosnecesitados@hotmail.com	https://www.facebook.com/manosalosnecesitados/?locale=es_LA	Migrant shelter

Mexico Resources

Cabo San Lucas, Baja California Sur

GOVERNMENT INSTITUTES				
Name	Address	Phone/Email	Website	Description
Cabo San Lucas City Government	Blvd Mijares N 1413, Entre Calle Zaragoza y Manuel Doblado, Col Centro 23400	(624) 146-7600 presidencia@loscabos.gob.mx	https://www.loscabos.gob.mx/	Job fairs, COVID-19 vaccine information, property tax payment
State Government of Baja California Sur	Blvd Mijares N 1413, Entre Calle Zaragoza y Manuel Doblado, Col Centro 23400	(624) 146-7600 presidencia@loscabos.gob.mx	https://www.loscabos.gob.mx/	Driver's license
Civil Registry	Jardines del Sol, 23475	(624) 143-3607	http://www.registro-civil.com.mx/baja-california-sur	Birth, marriage and death certificates
National Electoral Institute (INE)	Viaducto Tlalpan No 100 Col Arenal Tepepan, Alcaldía Tlalpan, CP 14610, Ciudad de México	(800) 433-2000	www.ine.mx	National ID card (INE)
Director of Municipal Transit	Carretera Transpeninsular Km 34, Col Guaymitas San José del Cabos	(624) 142-0361	http://transparencialoscabos.gob.mx/documentos/transparencia/fraccion-18/tramites/transito/expedicion-licencia-automovilista.pdf	Driver's license
Secretary of Public Education (SEP)	Blvd Luis Donaldo Colosio Esq Valentín Gómez Farias	(612) 123-8054 accesoalainformacionpublica@sepbcs.gob.mx	http://www.sepbcs.gob.mx/	Education at all levels, verification of US educational documents, English teacher positions
National Institute for Integral Family Development (DIF)	Calle Violetas s/n numero, Playa Caracoles, Col Jacarandas, 23473	(624) 184-6476	https://www.facebook.com/profile.php?id=100075984775479	A variety of services that include healthcare and food assistance, mental health and community services
Institute of Health for Well-Being (INSABI)	Various Locations		https://www.gob.mx/cms/uploads/attachment/file/512008/Baja_California_Sur.pdf	List of public hospitals and clinics
Mexican Institute of Social Security (IMSS)	Various Locations		http://www.imss.gob.mx/directorio/?page=589	Public hospital for workers at private companies

Mexico Resources

Cabo San Lucas, Baja California Sur

GOVERNMENT INSTITUTES				
Name	Address	Phone/Email	Website	Description
The Institute for Social Security Services for the Workers of the State (ISSSTE)	Calle Ignacio Zaragoza, Entre Alikan, 12 de Octubre y, Ildefonso Green, 23470		www.issste.gob.mx	Public hospital for state workers
Tax Administration Service (SAT)	Calle Adolfo Lopez 206, Matamoros, 23470	(800) 286-3133 contactovucem@sat.gob.mx; ventanillaunica@sat.gob.mx	https://citas.sat.gob.mx/	Federal tax collection, new business registration
Secretary of Foreign Relations (SRE)	Various Locations	(800) 801-0773	https://citas.sre.gob.mx/	Passport

NON-PROFIT ORGANIZATIONS				
Name	Address	Phone/Email	Website	Description
Mexican Red Cross	Delegacion Carretera Todos Santos, km 121	(624) 143-7869	https://www.cruzrojamexicana.org.mx/	24hr rescue/ambulance service
Casa Hogar	Calle Playas S/N entre Playa del Amor y Playa El Medano, Cerro de Los Venados, 23473 Cabo San Lucas	(624) 123-1285 info@casahogarcabo.com	https://www.casahogarcabo.com/	Housing/care for children/teens unable to live with families
La Paz Es Diversa	(612) 202-0703		https://www.facebook.com/lapazesdiversa/	

Mexico Resources

Puebla, Puebla

GOVERNMENT INSTITUTES				
Name	Address	Phone/Email	Website	Description
Puebla City Government	Ave 2 Pte 107	(222) 309-4300	https://www.pueblacapital.gob.mx/	Job fairs, COVID-19 vaccine information, property tax payment
Civil Registry	Various Locations		https://puebla.gob.mx/index.php/tramites-y-servicios?title=Registro%20Civil&cid=161	Birth, marriage and death certificates
National Electoral Institute (INE)	Various Locations	(222) 264-6729	www.ine.mx	National ID card (INE)
Secretary of Infrastructure, Mobility and Transport	Various Locations		https://citasenlinea.puebla.gob.mx/Default.aspx	Driver's license
Secretary of Public Education (SEP)	Av Jesús Reyes Heroles S/N, Colonia Nueva Aurora, 72070	(222) 229-6900	http://sep.puebla.gob.mx/	Education at all levels, verification of US educational documents, English teacher positions
National Institute for Integral Family Development (DIF)	Calle Cinco de Mayo 1606, Centro, 72000	(222) 229-5200 sedifestatal@puebla.gob.mx	http://difestatal.puebla.gob.mx/	A variety of services that include healthcare and food assistance, mental health and community services
Institute of Health for Well-Being (INSABI)	Calle 15 Sur 302, Barrio de San Sebastián, 72090	(222) 229-8300	http://ss.puebla.gob.mx/servicios/	List of public hospitals and clinics
Mexican Institute of Social Security (IMSS)	4 Norte 2055, Centro, 72000	(222) 246-3931	www.imss.gob.mx	Public hospital for workers at private companies
The Institute for Social Security Services for the Workers of the State (ISSSTE)	3 Poniente 1906, Amor, 72140	(222) 232-7994	www.issste.gob.mx	Public hospital for state workers

Mexico Resources

Puebla, Puebla

GOVERNMENT INSTITUTES				
Name	Address	Phone/Email	Website	Description
Secretary of Labor and Employment (STPS)	31 Poniente 2904, El Vergel, 72400	(222) 230-1670	www.stps.gob.mx	Job training and placement, worker protection
Secretaría de Salud del Estado de Puebla	Calle 6 Norte 603, Centro, 72000	(800) 581-4444	https://ss.puebla.gob.mx/	List of public hospitals and clinics
Tax Administration Service (SAT)	Various Locations		https://citas.sat.gob.mx/	Federal tax collection, new business registration
Secretary of Foreign Relations (SRE)	Vía Atlixcayotl 1101, Centro Integral De Servicios (CIS), Edificio Norte, Planta Baja, Col. Villas De Atlixco, 72190	(222) 467-1251	https://citas.sre.gob.mx/	Passport

NON-PROFIT ORGANIZATIONS				
Name	Address	Email	Website	Description
Tergar Meditation Community	Calle Huauchinango 40, La Paz, 72160	informacion@tergarpuebla.org	https://espanol.tergar.org/comunidades-y-grupos-de-practica/puebla/	Meditation community

ONLINE RESOURCES		
Name	Website	Description
Human Rights Commission's Migrant Services Directory	https://cdhpuebla.org.mx/v1/images/cartillas/8-DirectorioAtencionMigrantes2018.pdf	Migrant services directory

Mexico Resources

Guadalajara, Jalisco

HOTLINE		
Name	Address	Phone/Email
COVID-19 Hotline	(333) 823-3220	Hotline for people experiencing COVID-19 symptoms

GOVERNMENT INSTITUTES				
Name	Address	Phone/Email	Website	Description
Government of the City of Guadalajara	Hidalgo 400, Col. Centro, 44100	contacto@ guadalajara.gob. mx	https:// guadalajara.gob. mx	Job fairs, property tax payment
Civil Registry	Ave. Prolongación Alcalde 1855, Col. Miraflores, 44270, Planta Baja	(333) 819-2456 enrique. cardenas@ jalisco.gob.mx	https://sgg.jalisco. gob.mx/inicio	Birth, marriage, and death certificates
National Electoral Institute (INE)	Calle Francisco Rojas González 131, Ladron De Guevara, 44130	(800) 433 2000	https://app-inter. ife.org.mx/ siac2011/citas_ initCapturaCitas. siac	National ID card (INE)
Jalisco State Government	Ave. Fray Antonio Alcalde 1221, Col. Miraflores	(333) 668-1804	https://www. jalisco.gob.mx	Driver's license
National Employment Service (SNE)		(800) 841-2020	https://www. jalisco.gob.mx/es/ temas/portal-del- empleo	Government job placement agency that offers advice counseling for job placement
National Institute for Integral Family Development (DIF)	Various Locations	(333) 836-3444	https://difgdl.gob. mx/	A variety of services that include healthcare and food assistance, mental health and community services
Institute of Health for Well-Being (INSABI)	Dr. Baeza Alzaga 107, Col Centro		https://ssj.jalisco. gob.mx/	List of public hospitals and cities

Mexico Resources

GOVERNMENT INSTITUTES				
Name	Address	Phone/Email	Website	Description
Centro de Salud ACATIC	General Pablo Rodriguez 195, 45470	ssjtepa@prodigy.net.mx	https://ssj.jalisco.gob.mx	Public hospital
Centro de Salud El Chico	Francisco I Madero 37, Col. Centro, 48948	(333) 030-5000 regionautlan@gmail.com	https://ssj.jalisco.gob.mx	Public hospital
HGR 45 Guadalajara Hospital IMSS	Calle San Felipe 1014 Guadalajara, Col. Centro, 44100		http://www.imss.gob.mx/	Public hospital for workers at private companies
Hospital Regional Dr. Valentín Gómez Farias ISSSTE	Ave. Soledad Orozco 203, El Capullo, 45100, Zapopan	(333) 836 0650	https://www.gob.mx/issste?fbclid=IwAR2medaioz2c-gNBfoFa1qok2TzI3T50CLeBuJ_hbWUN45bHxdJ2HAra0u0	Public hospital for state workers
Tax Administration Service (SAT)	Calz. Lázaro Cárdenas 2305, Las Torres, 44920	(333) 880-9700	https://citas.sat.gob.mx/	Federal tax collection, new business registration
Secretary of Public Education (SEP)	Ave. Alcalde 1351, Magisterio, Col. Miraflores	(333) 819-2752	https://se.jalisco.gob.mx/	Education at all levels, verification of US educational documents, English teacher positions
Secretary of Labor and Social Welfare (STPS)	Calz. de las Palmas No. 96, Col. La Aurora, 44460	(333) 030-1000	https://stps.jalisco.gob.mx/	Job training and placement, worker protection
Secretary of Foreign Relations (SRE)	Villa Santa Rita, Ave. México 3370, Villas de San Javier, 44690	(331) 816-9003	https://citas.sre.gob.mx/	Passport

Guadalajara, Jalisco

NON-PROFIT ORGANIZATIONS				
Name	Address	Phone/Email	Website	Description
FM4 Paso Libre	Calderón de la Barca 468-A. Col. Arcos Vallarta, 44150	(333) 330-0306	https://fm4pasolibre.org/?lang=en	Serves food and basic supplies to Mexican and other migrants in transit. Limited access available for use of toilet and shower facilities
The Rhizome Center for Migrants		(332) 182-0836	https://www.rhizomecenter.org/es/	Supports and defends forcibly displaced persons and uprooted people at risk around the world. Through the help of technology and transborder networks, we combine direct services, advocacy, and socially-driven development to empower migrant communities
Casa Scalabrini Shelter		(333) 811-3342 cpmcs@yahoo.com	https://www.migrantes.com.mx/guadalajara	Provides shelter, addiction counseling and reintegration support to people who have been deported from the United States
Refugio Casa del Migrante	Constitución 300, Cerro del Cuatro, San Pedro Tlaquepaque, 45599	(333) 675-1475	https://www.elrefugiogdl.org.mx/	Offers food and shelter for migrants
Justice Center for Women (Centro de Justicia para las Mujeres)	Álvaro Alcázar 5869, Entre Ignacio Ramos y Circunvalación, Col. Jardines Alcalde	(333) 030-5450	https://fge.jalisco.gob.mx/	Offers psychological, legal, and basic medical care for women victims of domestic violence
CODISE A.C.	Juan Manuel 917, Zona Centro, 44100 Guadalajara, Jal., Mexico	(334) 008-5273 contacto@codise.org.mx	https://codise.org.mx/	

Mexico Resources

Monterrey, Nuevo Leon

GOVERNMENT INSTITUTES				
Name	Address	Phone	Website	Description
Monterrey City Government	Palacio Municipal de Monterrey, Zaragoza y Ocampo S/N, Centro, 64000	(818) 130-6565	http://www.monterrey.gob.mx/oficial/	Job fairs, COVID-19 vaccine information, property tax payment
Civil Registry	Various Locations	(812) 033-2880	https://www.nl.gob.mx/oficialiasderegistrocivil	Birth, marriage and death certificates
National Electoral Institute (INE)	Various Locations	(818) 345-8711	www.ine.mx	National ID card (INE)
Delegation of Vehicle Control Institute	Various Locations		http://retys.nl.gob.mx/servicios/licencia-de-conducir-para-automovilista-chofer-o-motociclista-expedicion	Driver's license
National Institute for Integral Family Development (DIF)	Loma Redonda 1500 Col Loma Larga	(815) 102-8600	https://www.facebook.com/DIFMonterrey-221260114722610/	A variety of services that include healthcare and food assistance, mental health and community services
Institute of Health for Well-being (INSABI)	Various Locations		https://www.gob.mx/insabi	List of public hospitals and clinics
Mexican Institute of Social Security (IMSS)	Manuel L Barragán 4850, Hogares Ferrocarrileros, 64260	(818) 351-5194	www.imss.gob.mx	Public hospital for workers at private companies
The Institute for Social Security Services for the Workers of the State (ISSSTE)	Degollado Sur 734, Obispado, 64060	(800) 400-1000	www.issste.gob.mx	Public hospital for state workers
Tax Administration Service (SAT)	Various Locations		https://citas.sat.gob.mx/	Federal tax collection, new business registration

Mexico Resources

Monterrey, Nuevo Leon

GOVERNMENT INSTITUTES

Name	Address	Phone	Website	Description
Secretary of Public Education (SEP)	Calle Nueva Jersey 4038, entre Nueva Irlanda y Nueva Australia, Fraccionamiento Industrial Lincoln, 64310	(818) 347-9432	https://www.nl.gob.mx/educacion	Education at all levels, verification of US educational documents, English teacher positions
Secretary of Labor and Employment (STPS)	General Lázaro Cárdenas 500, Mirador de La Silla, 67170 Guadalupe	(812) 020-2907	www.stps.gob.mx	Job training and placement, worker protection
Secretary of Foreign Relations (SRE)	Ave Eugenio Garza Sada Sur 2411, Roma, 64700	(812) 090-2501	https://citas.sre.gob.mx/	Passport

NON-PROFIT ORGANIZATIONS

Name	Address	Phone	Website
"Comedor de Los Pobres" Soup Kitchen	Calle 5 de Mayo S/N, Centro Monterrey, 64000	(818) 375-1163	http://www.comedordelospobres.org/
COMAC		info@comacmty.org	https://www.facebook.com/comacmty/?locale=es_LA

Part 6: Additional Resources

- Migrant App
- Sample Resume
- Sample Cover Letter
- Mexico Repatriation Site Directory
- Sample Job Application

MigrantApp, a Great Tool for Your Return

The MigrantApp, developed by the International Organization for Migrants (IOM), a UN Migration Agency, includes a number of features that may be of use to you:

- Protection and Assistance Information: Simplified access to information on health centers, consulates and embassies, migration offices, human rights protection centers, and shelters. The App also includes information on training and employment, and on assistance for particularly vulnerable groups, including victims of human trafficking.
- Migration Information: Information on the requirements for entering Mexico and Central American countries for 27 nationalities.
- Remittances: Allows you to compare the costs of available options for sending money.
- My Route: Allows you to privately share your location in real-time.
- News: Up-to-date, country-specific migration news and alerts in case of emergencies such as hurricanes and epidemics.

Your personal information is confidential, but you can also deactivate the GPS feature on your mobile device.

You can download the MigrantApp for Apple (iOS) or Samsung (Android).

Additional information on the MigrantApp is available on IOM's Mesoamerica Programme website: https://www.programamesoamerica.iom.int/es/migapp

Currículum Vitae

Nacido en los Estados Unidos Mexicanos el 14 de mayo de 1981
Avenida Hermanos Serdan 2390, Col. Centro
Puebla, Puebla, C.P. 72139
222-544-0928
RaulNavarro3@gmail.com

RAUL NAVARRO

RESUMEN DE EXPERIENCIA PROFESIONAL	Hablante nativo de inglés y español. Tengo cuatro años de experiencia enseñando inglés y un año de experiencia de asistente voluntario de enseñanza de matemáticas. Tengo experiencia aplicando diversas estrategias educativas en todos niveles.
EDUCACIÓN	**Diplomado en ciencias, el arte y la educación general** Carl Sandburg Community College Galesburg, IL Año: 2009
EXPERIENCIA PROFESIONAL DOCENTE	**Universidad de Illinois Urbana-Champaign , Programa de socios de lengua** Funciones: Maestro de inglés como segundo idioma (ESL), tutor de estudiantes Año: Agosto de 2014- Abril de 2016
VOLUNTARIADO	**Danville Area Community College** Danville, IL Funciones: Asistente voluntario de enseñanza de matemáticas, tutor de estudiantes Año: Julio de 2016- abril de 2018
IDIOMAS	Inglés lengua materna Español lengua materna
HONORES	Premio de liderazgo de John Dewey, Universidad de Illinois, Urbana-Champaign Año: 2014
CONOCIMIENTOS TECNOLÓGICOS	Microsoft Office: Word, PowerPoint, Excel

Carlos Rodríguez
C/ Roma, 10, 7º B
Ciudad de México

Programación Saturno SRL
Polígono Industrial Nuevo Campo, Edificio B

Ciudad de México, 30 de marzo de 2024

Estimados/as Sres/as,

Les escribo a ustedes para hacerles llegar mi interés por el puesto vacante de Programador Web. Hace dos años que finalicé mis estudios superiores de Ingeniería Informática en la universidad y desde entonces he estado desempeñando labores como desarrollador front-end en varias empresas de México y también de Estados Unidos.

La vacante de la oferta de trabajo me interesa particularmente por dos razones: son necesarias las mismas habilidades que domino desde hace años y creo que puedo aportar un valor añadido con mis recientes conocimientos de diseño en redes sociales.

Adicionalmente, también domino el desarrollo de aplicaciones multiplataforma, en especial Android, por lo que es una habilidad secundaria a tener en cuenta si lo consideran en un futuro.

Me gustaría concertar una entrevista para poder explicarles mis conocimientos con más detalle y mi gran interés por ocupar este puesto. Cualquier cosa que necesiten, estaré a su disposición en el método de contacto proporcionado en este correo electrónico y también en mi curriculum vitae. Quedo a la espera de su respuesta.

Un cordial saludo,
Carlos Rodríguez

[Firma]

DIRECTORIO ENLACES REPATRIACIÓN

Call Center: 800-2018542
Correo: attrepatriadascdmx@inami.gob.mx

Oficina de Representación	Nombre	Cargo	Teléfono	Conmutador: 555387-2400 extensión	Correo	Domicilio
Aguascalientes	Lic. Diana Guadalupe Íñiguez Pedroza	Jefa de Departamento de Asuntos Jurídicos	(449) 918 2464	8200 206	diniguez@ inami.gob.mx	Paseo de los Chicahuales No. 2790 int. 15, Col. Corral de Barrancos Jesús María, C.P. 20900, Aguascalientes, Aguascalientes
Baja California	Aidé Nereida Rosales Márquez	Subdirectora de Protección al Migrante	(664) 682 4038 Directo (664) 632 3218	60040	arosales@ inami.gob.mx	José María Larroque s/n, Col. Empleados Federales, C.P. 22010, Tijuana, Baja California.
Baja California Sur	Lic. Margarita Medina Mendoza	Jefa de Departamento de Informática	624-143-0135 ext. 203	8230 203	mmedinam@ inami.gob.mx	Boulevard Lázaro Cárdenas No. 1625, Col. Centro, Cabo San Lucas, C.P. 23050, Baja California Sur
Campeche	Matisse Geovana Alcalá Ortiz	Subdelegada Local en Campeche	(981) 816 2868 ext. 215	8250 215	malcala@ inami.gob.mx	Av. 16 de Septiembre s/n, Palacio Federal, Planta Baja, Col. Centro, C.P. 24000, San Francisco de Campeche, Campeche.
Chiapas	María Verónica Judith Brindis Ordaz	Jefa del Departamento de Control Migratorio y Enlace Paisano y Repatrición	(961)614 3288 (961) 614 3290 ext. 416	60416	vbrindis@ inami.gob.mx	Libramiento Norte Oriente s/n, costado de la Universidad Pablo Guardado Chávez, Col. Las Palmas, C.P. 29040, Tuxtla Gutiérrez, Chiapas.
Chihuahua	Melisa Cárdenas Baeza	Jefa del Módulo de Repatriación Humana Cd. Juárez	(656) 615 9858 (656) 612 3534	14180 14181	mcardenas@ inami.gob.mx	Puente Internacional Paso del Norte, Col. Centro, C.P. 32000, Cd. Juárez, Chihuahua.
Ciudad de México	Alejandrina Ortega Pichardo	Subdirectora del Programa de Repatriación Humana	(55) 53 87 24 00	18584 18144 32233	attrepatriadascdmx@ inami.gob.mx	Av. Homero 1832, Col. Los Morales Polanco, Miguel Hidalgo, C.P. 11510, Ciudad de México, CDMX.
Coahuila	María del Carmen Ramos Cruz	Jefa del Departamento de Informática y Enlace de Repatriación	(844) 416 1676 ext. 222	8330 222	mramos@ inami.gob.mx	Colima No. 213, esquina con Torreón, Col. República Oriente, C.P. 25280, Saltillo, Coahuila.

DIRECTORIO ENLACES REPATRIACIÓN

Call Center: 800-2018542
Correo: attrepatriadascdmx@inami.gob.mx

Oficina de Representación	Nombre	Cargo	Teléfono	Conmutador: 555387-2400 extensión	Correo	Domicilio
Colima	Ana Elizabeth Delgado Rivera	Coordinador de Unidad en Áreas de Servicios Migratorios	(314)332-1844 (314)332-1730 ext. 226	8350 226	edelgado@ inami.gob.mx	Av. Teniente Azueta s/n, Edificio Federal Portuario, 2do. Piso, Col. Burócrata, C.P. 28200, Manzanillo, Colima.
Durango	Claudia Azucena Carrola Cervantes	Jefa de Departamento del Programa Paisano	(618)825-0914 ext. 249	8360 249	ccarrola@ inami.gob.mx	Av. Belisario Domínguez No.134, entre Blvd. Dolores del Río y Calle Volantín, Barrio de Analco, C.P. 34138, Durango, Durango.
Estado de México	Azalia Catalina Camacho Guadarrama	Jefa de Departamento del Programa Paisano	(722)215-5880 ext. 220	8370 220	acamacho@ inami.gob.mx	Calle. Independencia No. 335, Delegación San Antonio Buenavista, C.P. 50266, Toluca, Estado de México.
Guanajuato	Francisco Antonio Camacho Rodríguez	Jefe de Departamento de Programa Paisano y Repatriación	(477) 713 55 90 (477) 713 55 92 ext. 61606	61606	fcamacho@ inami.gob.mx	Blvd. Aeropuerto No. 849, Col. Centro Comercial San Martín, Locales 106 E al 109 E, León, Guanajuato, C.P. 37545
Guerrero	Eva Lucrecia Agatón Catalán	Jefe de Departamento	(744) 435 0102 ext. 222	8390 222	eagaton@ inami.gob.mx	Juan Sebastián Elcano No. 1, Fracc. Costa Azul, C.P. 39850, Acapulco, Guerrero
Hidalgo	Héctor de Jesús Rodríguez de la Garza	Jefe del Departamento del Programa Paisano y Enlace de Repatriación	(771) 719 1374 (771) 719 3764 ext. 210 y 234	8410 210 8410 234	hrodriguez@ inami.gob.mx	Blvd. Ramón G. Bonfil No. 318, Col. Parque de Poblamiento, C.P. 42032, Pachuca de Soto, Hidalgo.
Jalisco	Eugenia Vignon Castrejón	Jefa de Departamento	(333)942 0290 Ext. 245 y 207	8420 245 8420 219 8420 207	evignon@ inami.gob.mx	Alcalde No. 500, 1er. piso, Edif. Palacio Federal, Col. Centro, Palacio Federal, C.P. 44280, Guadalajara, Jalisco.
Michoacán	Karina Hernández Cortés	Delegada Local en el Aeropuerto de la Ciudad de Morelia	(443)317 2348 directo	60711	khernandezc@ inami.gob.mx	Km. 27 Carretera Morelia - Zinapécuaro, Municipio de Álvaro Obregón, Michoacán C.P. 58920

DIRECTORIO ENLACES REPATRIACIÓN

Call Center: 800-2018542
Correo: attrepatriadascdmx@inami.gob.mx

Oficina de Representación	Nombre	Cargo	Teléfono	Ext.	Correo	Domicilio
Morelos	Miguel Ángel Becerra García	Jefe de Departamento de Programación, Informática y Estadística	(777)315 9610 (777)315 9611 opción 5	8460 212	mabecerra@ inami.gob.mx	Av. San Diego No. 101, esquina con Florencia, Col. Delicias,C.P. 62230, Cuernavaca, Morelos.
Nayarit	Beatriz Orozco Torres	Coordinadora de Unidad Especializada en Servicios Migratorios	(311)210 0773 (311)210 0774 (311) 213 1720 ext. 272	8470 272	borozcot@ inami.gob.mx	Av. Rey Nayar no. 171 esquina con Calle Miguel Lebrija, Col. Aviación, C.P. 63190, Tepic, Nayarit.
Nuevo León	Yolanda Álvarez Valdivia	Jefe de Departamento de Programa Paisano y Enlace de Repatriación	(818)486 1575 (818)486 1576 (818)486 1577 opción 7	8480 229	yalvarez@ inami.gob.mx	Av. Lázaro Cárdenas No. 1817, Fracc. Jardín de las Torres 1er. Sector, C.P. 64754, Monterrey, Nuevo León.
Oaxaca	Gladys Hernández Hernández	Jefa de Departamento	(951)502 0004 opción 4	8490 212	ghernandezh@ inami.gob.mx	Avenida de la Independencia No. 709, Palacio Federal, Col. Centro, C.P. 68000, Oaxaca de Juárez, Oaxaca.
Puebla	Lic. Humberto Garzón Gil	Jefe de Departamento de Programa Paisano y Enlace de Repatriación	(222)235 9043 ext. 251	8510 251	hgarzon@ inami.gob.mx	Av. Reforma, No. 1905 y 1907, Barrio San Matías, C.P. 72090, Puebla, Puebla.
Querétaro	Laura Itzigueri Ortega Gómez	Coordinador de Servicios Profesionales Especializados en Servicio Migratorio	(442)214 1538 ext. 204	8520 204	lortega@ inami.gob.mx	Prolongación Pino Suárez No. 479, Col. Ejido Modelo C.P. 76177 Querétaro, Qro.
Quintana Roo	Karen del Carmen Cupil Cupil	Jefa de Departamento	(998)881 3560 ext. 205	853 0205	kcupil@ inami.gob.mx	Av. Carlos Nader esquina con Av. Uxmal, Lote 1, Supermanzana 5, Col. Centro, C.P. 77500, Cancún, Quintana Roo.
San Luis Potosí	César Ricardo Soto Guzmán	Jefe de Departamento de Paisano y Enlace de Repatriación	(444)833 2481 ext. 222	8550 222	csoto@ inami.gob.mx	Av. Muñoz No. 362, Col. Los Reyes, C.P. 78165, San Luis Potosí, San Luis Potosí.

GOBERNACIÓN
SECRETARÍA DE GOBERNACIÓN

INM
SECRETARÍA DE GOBERNACIÓN
INSTITUTO NACIONAL DE MIGRACIÓN

REPATRIACIÓN
MÉXICO ESTÁ CONTIGO

DIRECTORIO ENLACES REPATRIACIÓN

Call Center: 800-2018542
Correo: attrepatriadascdmx@inami.gob.mx

Oficina de Representación	Nombre	Cargo	Teléfono	Ext.	Correo	Domicilio
Sinaloa	María Soledad García Zúñiga	Enlace de Comunicación Social, Programa Paisano y Repatriación	555387 2400 ext. 8560 224	8560 224	msgarciaz@ inami.gob.mx	Prol. Aquiles Serdán s/n, esq. con Playas Gemelas, Fracc. Playa Sur, C.P. 82040, Mazatlán, Sinaloa.
	María Fernanda Guzmán Guarneros	Jefa de Departamento Protección al Migrante	(667)717 8527	14631	fguzman@	Av. Independencia No. 833 Sur, Local 1-A, Col. Centro Sinaloa, C.P. 80000, Culiacán, Sinaloa
Sonora	Alejandrina Ortega Pichardo	Subdirectora del Programa de Repatriación Humana	(800)201 8542	32322	attrepatriadascd-mx@ inami.gob.mx	
Tabasco	Vidaura Magaña García	Jefa de Departamento	(993)313 6105 ext. 218 ó 227	8600 227	vmagana@ inami.gob.mx	Retorno Vía 5 No. 104, Planta Baja, Col. Tabasco 2000, C.P. 86035, Villahermosa, Tabasco.
Tamaulipas	Daniela Franco Vázquez	Jefe de Departamento de Programación, Informática y Estadística, Enlace Paisano y Repatriación	(867)712 1177 ext. 251	8620 251	dfranco@ inami.gob.mx	Av. Carlos César López de Lara, s/n, Col. Centro, C.P. 88000, Módulo Migración CITEV, Nuevo Laredo, Tamaulipas.
Tlaxcala	Ricardo Huerta González	Jefe de Departamento de Programación, Informática y Estadística	(246)464 0827 (246)464 0599 ext. 212	8640 212	rihuerta@ inami.gob.mx	Santos Degollado No. 62 en San Pablo Apetatitlán, C.P. 90600, Tlaxcala, Tlaxcala.
Veracruz	Saribel del Carmen Muñoz Pérez	Coordinadora de Unidad en Áreas de Servicios Migratorios	(229)989 7250 ext. 223	8650 223	smunoz@ inami.gob.mx	Miguel Lerdo No. 311, esq. 5 de Mayo, Col. Centro, C.P. 91700, Veracruz, Veracruz.
Yucatán	Virginia Alicia Franco Pérez	Jefa de Departamento	(999)925 5009 ext. 246	8670 246	vfranco@ inami.gob.mx	Calle 31 No. 94 entre 16 y 20, Col. México, C.P. 97125, Mérida, Yucatán
Zacatecas	Alma Carolina Gálvez de Ávila	Jefa de Departamento del Programa Paisano y Enlace de Repatriación	555387 2400 ext. 8680 200	8680 200	acgalvez@ inami.gob.mx	Av. Universidad No. 321 B, Col. La Loma, C.P. 98068, Zacatecas, Zacatecas.

Solicitud de Empleo

Puesto que Solicita	Fecha	
	Sueldo Mensual Deseado	
	Sueldo Mensual Aprobado	
Toda información aquí proporcionada debe ser tratada confidencialmente.	Fecha de Contratación	

Datos Personales

Apellino Paterno	Apellido Materno	Nombre(s)	Edad Años
Domicilio	Colonia	Codigo Postal	Telefono	Sexo ☐ Masculino ☐ Femenino
Ciudad, Estado	Lugar de Nacimiento		
		Fecha de Nacimiento	Nacionalidad
Vive con ☐ Sus Padres ☐ Su Familia ☐ Parientes ☐ Solo		Estatura	Peso
Personas que dependen de usted ☐ Hijos ☐ Cónyuge ☐ Padres ☐ Otros		Estado Civil ☐ Soltero ☐ Casado ☐ Otro	

Documentación

Clave Única de Registro de Población		Afore	
Reg. Fed. De Contribuyentes	Numero de Seguridad Social	Cartilla de Servicio Militar No.	Pasaporte No.
Tiene licencia de manejo ☐ No ☐ Si	Clase y Número de Licencia	Siendo extranjero que documentos le permiten trabajar en el país	

Estado de Salud y Habitos Personales

¿Como considera su estado de salud actual? ☐ Bueno ☐ Regular ☐ Malo		¿Padece alguna enfermedad crónica? ☐ No ☐ Si (Explique)
¿Práctica Ud. Algún Deporte?	¿Pertenece a un Club Social o Deportivo?	¿Cuál es su pasatiempo favorito?
¿Cuál es su meta en la vida?		

Datos Familiares

Nombre	Vive	Fin	Domicilio	Ocupación
Padre				
Madre				
Esposa (o)				
Nombre y Edades de los hijos				

Escolaridad

Nombre	Dirección	De	A	Años	Titulo Recibido
Primaria					
Secundaria o Prevocacional					
Preparatoria o Vocacional					
Profesional					
Comercial u Otras					

Estudios que esta cursando en la actualidad

Escuela: Horario: Curso o Carrera: Grado:

Conocimientos Generales

¿Que idiomas habla? (Nivel 50%, 75%, 100%)	Funciones de oficina que domina

Maquina de Oficina o taller que sepa manejar	Software que conoce
Otros trabajos o funciones que domina	

Empleo Actual y Anteriores

Concepto	Actual o último	Anterior	Anterior	Anterior
Tiempo que presto sus servicios	De a	De a	De a	De a
Nombre de la Compañía				
Dirección				
Teléfono				
Puesto desempeñado				
Sueldos Mensual				
Motivo de separación				
Nombre de su jefe directo				
Puesto de de jefe directo				

Podemos solicitar informes de usted	Comentarios de sus jefes
☐ Si	
☐ No (Razones)	

Referencias Personales (Favor de no incluir a jefes anteriores)

Nombre	Domicilio	Telefono	Ocupación	Tiempo de conocerlo

Datos Generales	Datos Económicos
¿Como supo de este empleo? ☐ Anuncio ☐ Otro medio (anótelo)	¿Tiene usted otros ingresos? Importe mensual ☐ No ☐ Si (descríbalos)
¿Tiene parientes trabajando en esta Empresa? ☐ No ☐ Si (nómbrelos)	¿Su cónyuge trabaja? Salario mensual ☐ No ☐ Si (¿dónde?)
¿Ha estado afianzado? ☐ No ☐ Si (nombre de la Cía.)	¿Vive en casa propia? Valor aproximado ☐ No ☐ Si
¿Ha estado afiliado a algún sindicato? ☐ No ☐ Si (¿a Cuál?)	¿Paga renta? Renta mensual ☐ No ☐ Si
¿Tiene seguro de vida? ☐ No ☐ Si (nombre de la Cía.)	¿Tiene automóvil propio? Marca Modelo ☐ No ☐ Si
¿Puede viajar? ☐ Si ☐ No (razones)	¿Tiene deudas? Importe ☐ No ☐ Si (¿con quién?)
¿Esta dispuesto a cambia de lugar de residencia? ☐ Si ☐ No (razones)	¿Cuanto abona mensualmente?
Fecha en que podría presentarse a trabajar	¿A cuánto ascienden sus gastos mensuales?

Comentarios del Entrevistador y Firma	Hago constar que mis respuestas son verdaderas
	Firma